The
Puerto
Rican
Americans

By Kate A. Conley

LUCENT BOOKS

An imprint of Thomson Gale, a part of The Thomson Corporation

THOMSON

™

GALE

Detroit • New York • San Francisco • San Diego • New Haven, Conn. • Waterville, Maine • London • Munich

LIBRARY OF CONGRESS CATALOGING-IN-PUBLICATION DATA

Conley, Kate A., 1977–
  The Puerto Rican Americans / by Kate A. Conley.
    p. cm. — (Immigrants in America)
  Includes bibliographical references and index.
  ISBN 1-59018-432-7 (hard cover : alk. paper)
Summary: The pioneer migration—The great migration—The "Puerto Rican problem"—The revolving door—A juggling act—An American success story.
  1. Puerto Ricans—United States—History—Juvenile literature. 2. Puerto Ricans—United States—Social conditions—Juvenile literature. 3. Immigrants—United States—History—Juvenile literature. 4. Puerto Rico—Emigration and immigration—History—Juvenile literature. 5. United States—Emigration and immigration—History—Juvenile literature. I. Title. II. Series.
  E184.P85C66 2005
  973'.04687295—dc22
                                                          2004026141

CONTENTS

FOREWORD

Immigrants have come to America at different times, for different reasons, and from many different places. They leave their homelands to escape religious and political persecution, poverty, war, famine, and countless other hardships. The journey is rarely easy. Sometimes, it entails a long and hazardous ocean voyage. Other times, it follows a circuitous route through refugee camps and foreign countries. At the turn of the twentieth century, for instance, Italian peasants, fleeing poverty, boarded steamships bound for New York, Boston, and other eastern seaports. And during the 1970s and 1980s, Vietnamese men, women, and children, victims of a devastating war, began arriving at refugee camps in Arkansas, Pennsylvania, Florida, and California, en route to establishing new lives in the United States.

Whatever the circumstances surrounding their departure, the immigrants' journey is always made more difficult by the knowledge that they leave behind family, friends, and a familiar way of life. Despite this, immigrants continue to come to America because, for many, the United States represents something they could not find at home: freedom and opportunity for themselves and their children.

No matter what their reasons for emigrating, where they have come from, or when they left, once here, nearly all immigrants face considerable challenges in adapting and making the United States

their new home. Language barriers, unfamiliar surroundings, and sometimes hostile neighbors make it difficult for immigrants to assimilate into American society. Some Vietnamese, for instance, could not read or write in their native tongue when they arrived in the United States. This heightened their struggle to communicate with employers who demanded they be literate in English, a language vastly different from their own. Likewise, Irish immigrant school children in Boston faced classmates who teased and belittled their lilting accent. Immigrants from Russia often felt isolated, having settled in areas of the United States where they had no access to traditional Russian foods. Similarly, Italian families, used to certain wines and spices, rarely shopped or traveled outside of New York's Little Italy, a self-contained community cut off from the rest of the city.

Even when first-generation immigrants do successfully settle into life in the United States, their children, born in America, often have different values and are influenced more by their country of birth than their parents' traditions. Children want to be a part of the American culture and usually welcome American ideals, beliefs, and styles. As they become more Americanized—adopting Western dating habits and fashions, for instance—they tend to cast aside or even actively reject the traditions embraced by their parents. Assimilation, then, often becomes an ideological dispute that creates conflict among immigrants of every ethnicity. Whether Chinese, Italian, Russian, or Vietnamese, young people battle their elders for respect, individuality, and freedom, issues that often would not have come up in their homeland. And no matter how tightly the first generations hold onto their traditions, in the end, it is usually the young people who decide what to keep and what to discard.

The Immigrants in America series fully examines the immigrant experience. Each book in the series discusses why the immigrants left their homeland, what the journey to America was like, what they experienced when they arrived, and the challenges of assimilation. Each volume includes discussion of triumph and tragedy, contributions and influences, history and the future. Fully documented primary and secondary source quotations enliven the text. Sidebars highlight interesting events and personalities. Annotated bibliographies offer ideas for additional research. Each book in this dynamic series provides students with a wealth of information as well as launching points for further discussion.

INTRODUCTION

The Puerto Rican Experience

Sixteen-year-old Ileana González was a young woman on a mission. Her first stop was the salon, where she had her fingernails painted red, white, and blue to match the Puerto Rican flag. Then she donned a blue dress with the words *Puerto Rico* sprawled across it in red lettering. Her final task was to gather family members and friends in order to secure a prime spot to view the event that had inspired her efforts in the first place: the Puerto Rican Day parade.

González is not alone in her enthusiasm for the parade. Each June for nearly fifty years, great crowds have lined Fifth Avenue in New York City. As the crowd chants "Boricua," which is an island term meaning "Puerto Rican," the parade begins snaking its way down the avenue. Within minutes New York City has been transformed into San Juan, complete with salsa music, miniature Puerto Rican flags, and beauty queens sitting atop floats. "This is the highlight of my year," says González. "To be proud of where you came from, it's the best."[1]

A Unique Situation

The Puerto Rican community that sponsors the parade in New York City is not new. It has been established for well over a century, beginning in earnest shortly after the

United States took possession of Puerto Rico at the end of the Spanish-American War in 1898. Since that time, Puerto Ricans have journeyed to the United States, like thousands of other immigrants from all over the world. They have come in three distinct waves: the Pioneer Migration (1900–1945), the Great Migration (1946–1964), and the Revolving-Door Migration (1965–present).

While Puerto Ricans have arrived just as other immigrants did, they are a distinct group in many ways. Most notably, all Puerto Ricans, whether they live on the island or the mainland, are U.S. citizens. They do not have to complete a residency requirement, take an American civics test, undergo a background check, or swear an oath of allegiance like other immigrants who want to become citizens. They automatically have the rights and responsibilities granted to U.S. citizens once they arrive on the mainland.

Puerto Ricans also differ from many immigrant groups, especially those from distant lands, in maintaining very close ties to their homeland. These close ties have allowed Puerto Ricans to keep alive their island traditions, remain active in the debate over the political status of the island, and avoid total assimilation into mainstream

Each year, crowds of Puerto Rican Americans line New York City's Fifth Avenue to celebrate their island heritage during the city's Puerto Rican Day parade.

American culture. It has produced a type of bicultural identity that is part Puerto Rican and part American.

Geography has played a large role in keeping the ties between migrants and the island strong. Puerto Rico is only about one thousand miles southeast of Miami, Florida. This short distance means round-trip flights are generally inexpensive and quick, so Puerto Ricans on the mainland can travel to the island to visit friends and family frequently and affordably.

Another reason Puerto Ricans have been able to maintain their close ties to the island has nothing to do with geography and everything to do with their motivation for moving. Unlike other immigrants, Puerto Ricans have never had to flee religious persecution, cruel dictators, wars, or famines. Instead, the majority came to find work, and many dreamed of returning to the island as soon as they had earned enough money. Statistics have repeatedly shown that when the unemployment rate is high on the island, the rate of migration to the mainland increases. The trend also works in reverse: When jobs become more plentiful on the island, Puerto Ricans on the mainland return there.

Overcoming Obstacles

Clearly, Puerto Ricans are different from other immigrants. They have the benefit of U.S. citizenship and easy access to their homeland.

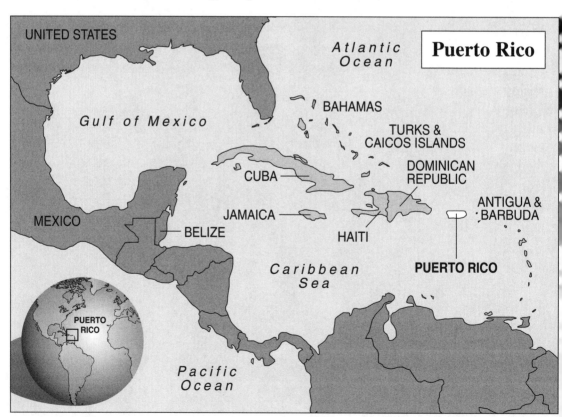

These advantages, however, have not exempted Puerto Ricans from the difficulties of assimilating to life in mainstream America. In fact, the experiences of Puerto Ricans in the United States are distinctly those of an immigrant population. Like other immigrants, Puerto Ricans have faced discrimination, often based on negative stereotypes, and a language barrier. Moreover, as their community in New York City grew during the 1950s, it became a scapegoat for the city's ills, resulting in additional hardships.

These difficulties caught many Puerto Ricans off guard. They were, after all, U.S. citizens, and they expected to be treated as such. Herman Badillo, who in 1970 became the first Puerto Rican–born U.S. congressman, reflects on this situation:

> The Puerto Rican has, until just recently, generally been relegated to second-class citizenship and has had to struggle against seemingly insurmountable odds. Unlike other immigrants of earlier years, Puerto Ricans are already United States citizens. Nevertheless, they are often denied the full advantages of such status

and have experienced the greatest difficulty in being assimilated into the American manner of life.[2]

Despite these difficulties, in the past century Puerto Ricans have become well established in the United States. Leaders have emerged from the Puerto Rican community, achieving success in a wide variety of fields ranging from music and drama to journalism and politics. All the while, Puerto Rican communities have remained true to their island heritage by preserving traditional food, music, dances, and the Spanish language.

Today, the Puerto Rican community in the United States is thriving. According to the 2000 Census, approximately half of all Puerto Ricans—about 3.4 million people—live in the United States. They have established their homes and businesses across the nation, from urban areas such as New York City to small towns such as Collegeville, Pennsylvania. In 1999 Roberto Clemente Jr., son of the legendary Puerto Rican baseball player, spoke for many when he said, "It's a very good thing to be Puerto Rican right now."[3]

CHAPTER ONE

The Pioneer Migration

At the dawn of the twentieth century, Puerto Rico was in a state of transition. For 405 years, the island had been a Spanish colony. That all changed on July 25, 1898, when U.S. troops landed at the costal town of Guánica, Puerto Rico. The landing was part of a military campaign during the Spanish-American War, and in just eighteen days U.S. troops seized control of the island from Spanish forces. Puerto Rico officially became a U.S. possession at the war's end, when Spanish and American officials signed the Treaty of Paris in December 1898.

Adjusting to life under new leadership was a major challenge for Puerto Ricans during this time period, when nearly every familiar aspect of society began to change. Teachers were trained to give lessons to students in English rather than Spanish. The island's currency was changed from the Spanish peso to the U.S. dollar. Even the spelling of the island's name was temporarily replaced with a more Americanized version, "Porto Rico."

As American lawmakers began making decisions about the island's future and job opportunities became plentiful on the mainland, many Puerto Ricans began to settle in the United States. The first major wave of Puerto Ricans that moved to the mainland is referred to as the Pioneer Migration. It lasted from 1900 to 1945, and with it came the beginning of a growing and vibrant Puerto Rican community in the United States.

Discontent Spreads

Not long after the Treaty of Paris was signed, members of the U.S. Congress began passing legislation on the newly acquired island of Puerto Rico. The Foraker Act of April 1900 established a system of government under which Puerto Ricans had very limited control. While Puerto Ricans would have the right to elect a resident commissioner to represent them in Congress, he could not vote. In addition, the island's top official—the governor—would be appointed by the U.S. president, leaving Puerto Ricans without a voice in determining their leader.

The Foraker Act did more than establish Puerto Rico's new government, however. It also settled upon a status for the island: unincorporated territory. The status was new in American history, and it created a gray area in terms of how Puerto Ricans fit into the United States. They were denied U.S. citizenship, but they were required to follow all

After the United States seized control of Puerto Rico in 1898, American administrators opened new schools, like this one in Caguas, in which English was the language of instruction.

U.S. laws. The rights granted under the U.S. Constitution did not apply to them.

The Foraker Act left many Puerto Ricans disillusioned with the United States and its role on the island. In 1909, leaders of a prominent political party called the Union of Puerto Rico decided to draw attention to the island's discontent. They led a peaceful rebellion by refusing to pass a budget for the following year. They also accused the island's American governor, Regis Post, of preventing local lawmakers from acting on the wishes of the people.

Although the crisis was resolved peacefully, the issue of U.S. control over Puerto Rico had surfaced. The island's leaders explored possible approaches to this matter, which included gaining greater self-rule, achieving independence, and requesting that the island become a state. The leaders were divided about the island's future, and the ongoing discussion, known as the status debate, would continue for the next century. Everyone agreed on one issue, however: Puerto Rico should never be a colony again.

On to Hawaii

The controversial Foraker Act affected more than the island's status and government. It also extended into the world of business by creating free trade between the United States and Puerto Rico. To capitalize on this arrangement, American sugar companies began buying vast tracts of land in Puerto Rico. Aware of the island's ready supply of experienced sugarcane laborers, American sugar companies also began recruiting Puerto Ricans to work on their plantations in the U.S. territory of Hawaii.

According to Charles Allen, Puerto Rico's governor from 1900 to 1901, the American recruiters "penetrated the rural districts and offered golden inducements to these simple folk to travel and see foreign lands. Laborers are wanted in Hawaii to work the sugar fields. . . . Good wages are offered, and many are persuaded to emigrate."[4] In late 1900 the first group of Puerto Ricans left for Hawaii. It included 114 men, women, and children.

The group faced a six-thousand-mile journey that began when they boarded a ship in Puerto Rico. From there they sailed to New Orleans, where they took a train that transported them to San Francisco. From San Francisco they boarded their final ship, which took them all the way to Honolulu. Many abandoned the daunting journey, especially after enduring shortages of water and food, and only 56 of the original 114 Puerto Ricans arrived in Hawaii.

The difficult travel conditions did little to discourage others on the island from going to Hawaii, however. Between 1900 and 1901 more than five thousand Puerto Ricans made the journey. They found work on several of the Hawaiian islands, including Maui, the Big Island, and Oahu. However, few of the Puerto Ricans found the working conditions or the pay as wonderful as the recruiters had promised. An article that appeared in the *New York World* in 1901 revealed the harsh conditions the workers faced:

A story of suffering and misery is told by the laborer Juan Avilés who was brought to these isles to work in the canefields. Avilés is a boy of eighteen, one of the first Puerto Ricans to emi-

A team of Puerto Rican farmhands loads sugarcane onto a cart. American sugar companies recruited Puerto Rican sugarcane laborers to work on their Hawaiian plantations.

grate to this country. The agents who contracted him had promised him earnings of $18.00 a month, but once he got here they only gave him $15.00. When he became so ill that he was no longer useful on the job, they let him go. . . . He spent his days wandering through the city picking in trash cans for something to eat. One day he dropped dead of hunger in a doorway. They say his condition was no worse than that of others who are still working. They, also, cannot survive on what they are earning.[5]

Choosing New York City

Not all of the Puerto Ricans who left their homeland in search of better economic conditions moved to Hawaii. A far greater number decided to settle on the mainland, and their destination of choice was New York.

Los Tabaqueros

In the years before World War I, tabaqueros *accounted for approximately 60 percent of all Puerto Ricans living in New York. They brought with them a tradition of education and political activism. At the root of this tradition was the reader. As the* tabaqueros *worked, the reader recited the works of authors ranging from Karl Marx to Victor Hugo. In his memoir, Bernardo Vega describes the readings at El Morito factory in New York:*

During the readings at "El Morito" and other factories, silence reigned supreme—it was almost like being in church. Whenever we got excited about a certain passage we showed our appreciation by tapping our tobacco cutters on the work tables. . . . At the end of each session there would be a discussion of what had been read. Conversation went from one table to another without our interrupting our work. Though nobody was formally leading the discussion, everyone took turns speaking. When some controversy remained unresolved and each side would stick to a point of view, one of the more educated workers would act as arbiter. And should dates or questions of fact provoke discussion, there was always someone who insisted on going to the *mataburros* or "donkey-slayers"—that's what we called reference books.

Although other states were closer to the island, they had relatively few job opportunities for unskilled and semiskilled workers. In Florida, for example, a large population of Cuban immigrants had saturated the labor market. The same situation was occurring in Texas as Mexican immigrants crossed the Rio Grande in increasing numbers. As a result, Puerto Ricans in search of jobs trekked up the Atlantic Coast to New York City.

New York City was also an attractive destination for Puerto Rican immigrants because there were already Puerto Rican enclaves there. A small number of Puerto Rican *tabaqueros* (cigar makers) and revolutionaries had come to New York City when Spain ruled the island. The small but established community in New York City made the transition to the United States easier for the new arrivals. The Spanish-speaking city dwellers were able to help the newcomers find places to live and work.

Beyond that, New York City also held another advantage for Puerto Ricans: It was an economical place to travel to. Although steamships traveled from San Juan, Puerto Rico, to southern cities such as New Orleans, Tampa, and Galveston, the passage took more than two weeks and was quite costly. Steamers that traveled from San Juan to New York, on the other hand, were more affordable and the trip generally took only four to five days.

From San Juan to New York

Although the journey from Puerto Rico to New York was much shorter than what immigrants from Europe and Asia experienced, the voyage was nonetheless filled with anticipation and excitement. Bernardo Vega, a Puerto Rican who immigrated to the United States in 1916 aboard the ship *Coamo,* described the mood among the passengers during his voyage to New York:

> The days passed peacefully. Sunrise of the first day and passengers were already acting as though they belonged to one family. It was not long before we came to know each other's life stories. The topic of conversation, of course, was what lay ahead: life in New York. First savings would be for sending for close relatives. Years later the time would come to return home with pots of money. Everyone's mind was on that farm they'd be buying or the business they'd set up in town. . . . All of us were building our own little castles in the sky. [6]

The immigrants, filled with excitement and nervousness, took in the sights of New York City as their ships approached the mainland. Minerva Torres Ríos, who arrived on the ship *Coamo* just a few years after Vega did, recalled her first impressions of her new homeland:

> When we reached New York harbor, it was winter and the pier was hidden in fog. We had to wait for two more days outside the port for the weather to clear. Finally the ship sailed into the harbor, and we crossed in front of the Statue of Liberty and you can imagine what an impression that made on me. . . . The Statue of Liberty was the first marvel I experienced in the City of Skyscrapers. When we disembarked on the Brooklyn pier it was very cold, and I saw another wonder for the first time: snow. I knew what it was, of course, from studying the history of the United States, but I had never seen it personally and to see the ground all covered in white astonished me. [7]

Once on U.S. soil, Torres Ríos, Vega, and thousands of other Puerto Ricans faced the challenging process of getting settled in a new country. Their first priorities were finding a place to live and securing a job. These two tasks went hand in hand, and most Puerto Rican immigrants chose to settle in neighborhoods that offered the best opportunities for work.

During the early part of the century, many Puerto Ricans settled in Brooklyn near the Navy Yard, where jobs were easy to find along the waterfront. A large number of the Puerto Rican immigrants were experienced *tabaqueros,* just like those who had arrived in the United States before the Spanish-American War. These skilled workers chose to settle in parts of Manhattan where hundreds of cigar factories were located: Chelsea and the Lower East Side, as well as the city's West Side.

Citizenship Draws Puerto Ricans to America

As Puerto Rican immigrants worked to establish themselves on the mainland, Puerto

Ricans on the island continued to seek greater self-rule. Congress finally addressed their concerns in 1916 when it began discussing the Jones Act. The proposed act would provide Puerto Ricans with a bill of rights and greater local rule. More significantly, it would grant U.S. citizenship to Puerto Ricans.

In March 1917 President Woodrow Wilson signed the Jones Act into law. Puerto Ricans had a window of six months to renounce citizenship. Doing so would result in ineligibility to vote or hold office, as well as limitations on other civil rights. Of the island's 1.2 million people, only 288 did not accept U.S. citizenship.

Once the Jones Act passed and Puerto Ricans became citizens, moving to the United States became far easier for them. Because they were already citizens, Puerto Ricans did not have to endure the medical exams, background checks, and other entry requirements other immigrants faced. In fact, moving from the island to the mainland was considered the same as moving from one state to another. So from this point forward, Puerto Ricans were considered migrants rather than immigrants.

The ease of moving to the United States encouraged many Puerto Ricans to do just that, and the number of migrants increased significantly. Before the Jones Act, the largest number of Puerto Ricans to move to the United States had done so between 1909 and 1916, when 7,394 Puerto Ricans arrived upon U.S. shores. After the Jones Act passed in 1917, 10,812 Puerto Ricans left the island in that single year alone. Just three years later, Puerto Ricans were reported to live in forty-five of the forty-eight states.

Economic Opportunities

Ease of settlement was not the only factor motivating Puerto Rican migration. Puerto Ricans were also looking for better job opportunities. The island's economy had undergone a major shift during the years following the Spanish-American War. Traditionally, Puerto Rico's main crops had been sugarcane, tobacco, and coffee. Workers had cultivated and processed each crop seasonally. When American investors arrived, they focused on sugarcane cultivation almost exclusively. When sugarcane was out of season, many Puerto Rican workers found themselves jobless and broke. The United States began to look like an attractive option.

The economic boom occurring on the mainland during the 1920s provided many job opportunities for Puerto Rican migrants. This good fortune was further bolstered in 1921, 1924, and 1929, when members of Congress passed acts that restricted the number of immigrants allowed into the United States. As U.S. citizens, Puerto Ricans were unaffected by these acts and were able to fill the jobs that had typically been held by immigrants from Europe and Asia. Many Puerto Ricans found work in factories, where jobs required little experience and limited English skills. Others found work as household servants, laundry workers, or day laborers at construction sites.

The demand for workers was so strong in the 1920s that many American businesses recruited Puerto Ricans to work in their American shops and factories. One such business was the American Manufacturing Company, which was located in Brooklyn's Greenpoint neighborhood. This company was the second-largest employer in Brooklyn, and its representatives recruited 130 Puerto Rican women to work at its rope-making factory.

The American Manufacturing Company paid for the women's steamship passage to New York. Once the women arrived, their new employers provided them with modern housing, free bus service to and from work, and chaperones to oversee their welfare in the city. In this way, the American Manufacturing Company and many other businesses like it were responsible for employing and settling hundreds of early Puerto Rican migrants.

Not all Puerto Ricans learned of the employment opportunities on the mainland through corporate recruiting, however. Many people got word of available jobs through personal letters. As Puerto Ricans settled in the United States, they would write home describing their high wages and good jobs. Hearing this from a trusted family member or friend enticed many Puerto Ricans to take the risk and migrate to the United States themselves.

A family of sugarcane workers poses in front of their miserable hut. Throughout the 1920s, many Puerto Ricans migrated to the United States in search of better opportunities.

Colonias

As migration from the island continued, distinctly Puerto Rican neighborhoods called *colonias* began to develop. According to estimates by the *New York Times* and the New York Mission Society, by 1926, *colonias* in New York City were home to between 150,000 and 200,000 Puerto Ricans. During that time, East Harlem had the largest *colonia,* which came to be known as El Barrio or Spanish Harlem. It was home to about 80 percent of the city's Puerto Rican population, and for this reason it became known as *la cuna de la comunidad* (the cradle of the community).

El Barrio and *colonias* like it provided a framework that allowed the migrants to remain close to family members, friends, and neighbors from the island. This fostered a sense of community. It was common, for example, for large groups of family members and neighbors to gather to celebrate birthdays, weddings, and holidays. It was also common for families who had large apartments to host parties where people spent the night listening to poetry and dancing to traditional Puerto Rican music coming from a hand-cranked record player called a Victrola.

Life in the *colonias* was not just about having parties and dancing, however. In El Barrio, as well as other *colonias,* Puerto Ricans established businesses to serve their community. Some of the earliest and most successful of these ventures were small grocery stores, or *bodegas.* They specialized in ingredients for traditional Puerto Rican meals, such as rice, beans, and plantains. Like *bodegas, botánicas* were also quickly established in the *colonias.* These stores sold medicinal plants, as well as items for devotional use. Puerto Rican restaurants, bakeries, barbershops, and other businesses soon joined the *bodegas* and *botánicas* as the *colonias* grew.

Learning English

For those who acquired fluency in English, navigating outside the *colonias* was much easier. Doña Petra Negrón, like so many other Puerto Rican migrants, worked hard to learn English when she arrived in the United States. Though she had enrolled in an American high school and was learning English quickly, she had to quit in order to get a job.

While she worked as a packer in a candy factory, Doña Petra's desire to learn English grew. In *From Colonia to Community,* author Virginia E. Sánchez Korrol quotes Doña Petra's explanation: "Can you imagine what a lonely feeling; to have people speak to you and not to understand and not be able to communicate in everyday situations? From that time on I purposely set out to get a command of the language (*a la brava aprendí el inglés*). Within a short time, I was able to defend myself in English and then . . . [I] took the newcomers to the city in search of jobs, houses, or whatever."

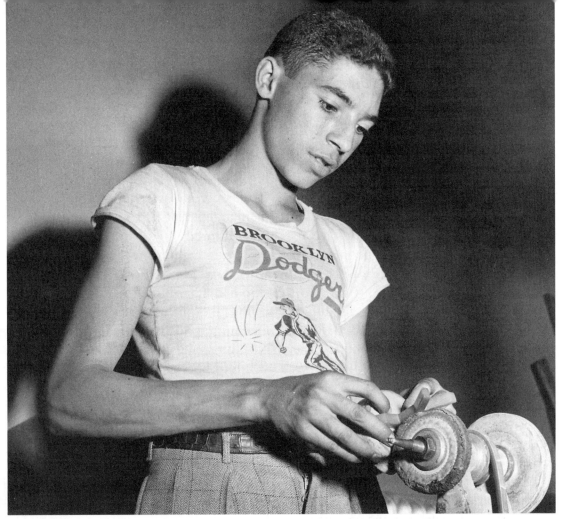

A young Puerto Rican man in New York sands a piece of wood in a carpenter's shop. Many Puerto Rican immigrants took jobs that involved simplistic, repetitive labor.

Many of the businesses operating in the *colonias* were listed in the *Guía Hispana,* which was similar to a telephone book. It was one of many Spanish-language publications created for the community. Although many Puerto Ricans could speak at least some English, Spanish was the language they preferred to use with friends and family. It was a bond that united the community, as well as a link to the island.

Clubs, associations, and organizations also served to bond the community. Puerto Ricans founded several community groups that provided a number of services, from sponsoring lectures to aiding the needy. The Porto Rican Brotherhood of America, established in 1923, was one of the most active organizations. Its members organized dances, held fund-raisers for the community, and acted as advocates for Puerto Ricans facing legal problems.

The Harlem Riots

In July 1926 the Porto Rican Brotherhood got involved in peacekeeping efforts during what became known as the Harlem Riots. That summer, New York City experienced a brutal heat wave. Seeking relief from their crowded, non-air-conditioned apartments, Puerto Ricans began spending more time outdoors and even took to sleeping on their fire escapes and rooftops. Tensions escalated between Puerto Ricans and other Harlem residents, and before long arguments led to street fights. More than fifty people were wounded and several *bodegas* were vandalized.

The *New York Times,* using language that today sounds somewhat biased, identified the root of the Harlem Riots as "the rapid influx of Latins and West Indian negroes who describe themselves as Porto Ricans. The newcomers have opened their own stores and patronize no others. The old residents of the district have resented the invasion."[8]

Tension between the established residents of Harlem and the newer Puerto Rican migrants extended beyond commerce. Many Puerto Ricans, who were descended from African slaves or the Taíno Indians native to the island, had dark skin and faced racial prejudice from some of Harlem's white residents. The situation was further aggravated by the fact that Puerto Ricans were free to enter the United States at a time when other immigrants were restricted. Many older Harlem residents were immigrants themselves, and they believed it was an injustice to bar their skilled family members from immigration while simple *jíbaros* (peasant farmers) from Puerto Rico could come whenever they pleased.

Facing Discrimination

Discrimination against Puerto Ricans extended well beyond the events during the summer of the Harlem Riots. For example, some Puerto Ricans found that boardinghouses refused to rent to them. While walking along an uptown street in Manhattan, Bernardo Vega saw a sign that read: "Apartment to let. No Cubans, Puerto Ricans, or dogs allowed."[9]

Discrimination was also present in the workplace. Many Puerto Ricans with dark skin had a hard time getting hired, especially if they did not speak English fluently. One migrant, Rosa Roma, addressed this type of racial discrimination by saying, "If you looked Irish or German [rather than Puerto Rican] it didn't matter how limited your English was. Most jobs were on assembly lines and it didn't take much talking to learn the procedure."[10]

Some discrimination Puerto Ricans faced, however, reflected mainstream America's widespread ignorance about the island. Even though Puerto Rico had been tied to the United States since 1898, during the period of the Pioneer Migration "some educated Americans still wanted to know how to drive to Puerto Rico and others sent the [Puerto Rican] governor letters addressed to 'San Juan, Puerto Rico, Philippine Islands, U.S.A.'"[11]

Despair on the Island

As Puerto Ricans on the mainland struggled to find their place in the melting pot of New York society, their friends and family living on the island fared poorly. In 1928 Hurricane San Felipe ripped across parts of Puerto Rico. It killed hundreds of people, left more than seven hundred thousand residents homeless, and destroyed the island's crops. Just as Puerto Ricans were recovering from San Felipe, Hurricane San Ciprián hit the island in 1932, bringing even more death and devastation.

As if the hurricanes had not done enough damage to Puerto Rico, the Great Depression reached the island in the 1930s. The troubled economy combined with the disastrous hurricanes created a dire situation, and poverty was widespread. According to the island's governor, Theodore Roosevelt Jr., Puerto Rico contained

farm after farm where lean underfed women and sickly men repeated again and again the same story—little food and no opportunity to get more. . . . I have watched in a classroom thin, pallid little boys and girls trying to spur their brains to action when their little bodies were underfed. I have seen them trying to study on only one scanty meal a day, a meal of a few beans and some rice. I have looked into the kitchen of houses where a handful of beans and a few plantains were the fare for the entire family.[12]

By December 1934 the situation in Puerto Rico had become desperate. The powerful Puerto Rican political leader Luis Muñoz Marín warned President Franklin D. Roosevelt that something had to be

This photo from 1934 captures the deplorable living conditions of a San Juan slum. Puerto Rico was particularly hard hit by the Great Depression of the 1930s.

done. According to Muñoz Marín, "Public order hangs today by a thread."[13] Indeed, it didn't take long for violence to break out.

Under the leadership of Pedro Albizu Campos, Puerto Rico's pro-independence Nationalist Party began taking center stage. The party became an outlet for the islanders' frustration and anti-American sentiments, and nationalist demonstrations quickly led to a number of deaths. When two nationalists killed Elisha Riggs, an American police chief working on the island, it appeared that U.S. lawmakers would reexamine Puerto Rico's status. In April 1936 the Tydings Bill was introduced to U.S. lawmakers. It proposed granting independence to the island as soon as possible. The bill quickly died in Congress, however, and violence continued in Puerto Rico.

Throughout the 1930s, Puerto Rican nationalist Pedro Albizu Campos led the island's fight for independence from the United States.

Returning to Puerto Rico

Amid the island's violence and poverty—indeed, because of it—Puerto Rican migration to the United States continued throughout the 1930s and 1940s. Many migrants were disappointed when they arrived in America, however. Like the island, the mainland was suffering from an economic depression, and jobs were scarce.

As Puerto Ricans realized that jobs were no longer plentiful, the rate of migration slowed. During this time, thousands of Puerto Ricans decided to leave New York and return to the island. One migrant who left in 1937 expressed his reason for returning by stating, "We are very disappointed with New York. We thought this was the money center of the world."[14]

In addition to the economic distress, many Puerto Ricans had a difficult time adjusting to a new climate and city. New York's blustery winters were a sharp contrast to the island's tropical weather. One Puerto Rican who chose to return to the island struck upon this idea by saying, "I never want to see a fur coat again. I just want little clothes and warm sun."[15] Beyond the harsh climate, many migrants who were from rural parts of Puerto Rico found it dif-

Wartime Migration

German submarines lurking in waters of the Caribbean during the war made migration from Puerto Rico to the United States more dangerous than ever. In Memoirs of a Visionary, *Antonia Pantoja, who migrated aboard the SS* Florida *in 1944, describes these conditions:*

I made friends with other passengers and the soldiers. . . . There were about two hundred American soldiers and fifty civilians on board. We learned from the soldiers that our ship was one of the convoys that traveled from Puerto Rico to Guantánamo, Cuba. They also informed us that the highly visible dark spots on the water were oil slicks from ships that had been sunk by German submarines that were very active in these waters. Much to my amazement, I did not feel any fear about our safety during the trip. Exploring the ship and talking with the soldiers, I learned that a large portion of our ship carried war equipment. I also noticed that we always had one ship in front of us and one behind us. . . . In Guantánamo, other cargo ships and an air blimp joined us.

ficult to adjust to the city's noise, pollution, and fast-paced lifestyle.

World War II

As the Great Depression continued to plague the United States and Puerto Rico, World War II began in Europe. Then, on December 7, 1941, Japanese forces led a surprise attack on Pearl Harbor, Hawaii, and the United States was drawn into the war. A demand for workers quickly arose in the United States as the nation entered the war, and Puerto Rican migrants traveled to the mainland to fill the newly created jobs.

As the war progressed, life on the island was growing more difficult. German submarines were patrolling the Caribbean Sea near Puerto Rico, and hundreds of Puerto Rican sailors died when German submarines destroyed their merchant ships. A submarine blockade later prevented ships from docking at San Juan Harbor for months at a time and food shortages became a terrible problem on the island.

Conditions on the island were so alarming that New York Representative Vito Marcantonio, whose district included a vast number of Puerto Rican migrants, addressed Congress about Puerto Rico's problems. He said, "On the island there are 325,000 unemployed. . . . Food is scarce. There is no rice, beans, or codfish, all staples in the native diet. The cost of living has risen over 175 percent above normal. . . . I suggest that Puerto Rican workers be brought to the United States to work under decent conditions." [16]

Like Marcantonio, many Puerto Ricans saw the United States as a place of refuge. By the war's end in 1945, the United States was on the verge of receiving the largest wave of Puerto Rican migrants to date.

CHAPTER TWO

The Great Migration

"I came to New York because the food situation was very bad in Puerto Rico and there was no work. One of my sisters who lived in San Juan, the capital, went to New York. She sent for my brother first. Later I came with my father,"[17] says one migrant who settled in the United States shortly after World War II ended. Another describes his reasons for migrating by saying, "There is nothing in Puerto Rico. My father and brothers are here [in the United States]. I don't like it here but I hate it there. Here at least I can survive."[18]

These two migrants were joined by thousands of others seeking better living conditions and new job opportunities on the mainland. Such a vast number of Puerto Ricans migrated between 1946 and 1964 that these years are known as the Great Migration. During this period more than 550,000 Puerto Ricans—roughly a quarter of the island's total population—migrated to the United States. It was the largest number of Puerto Rican migrants to travel to U.S. shores in the nation's history. These years also brought changes to relations between the island and the mainland, and the two groups continued to seek resolution to the status debate.

After the War

World War II drew to a close in September 1945, and within weeks the process of refining the relationship between Puerto Rico and the United States resumed with renewed vigor. Just a month after the war's end, President Harry S. Truman asked Congress to consider a plebiscite for Puerto Rico. The plebiscite would be an opportunity for Puerto Ricans to vote for one of four options for the future of the island: greater self-rule, statehood, independence, or a combination of self-rule and a continued association with the United States.

The ongoing discussions in Congress led Puerto Rico's governor, Rexford Tugwell, to believe it would still be years before Puerto Ricans were granted enough self-rule to elect their own leader. So before Congress could act, Tugwell resigned and asked Truman to appoint a Puerto Rican—rather than an American—as the island's next governor. It would be a compromise of sorts: The United States would still determine who led the island, but at the same time the leader would be someone who, as a native of the island, understood Puerto Rico as no mainland American could. Truman acted on Tugwell's

In this photo from 1950, Puerto Rican migrants line up to board a plane bound for Michigan. After World War II, nearly one quarter of the island's population migrated to the United States.

idea, and in 1946 he appointed Jesús Piñero as the island's first Puerto Rican–born governor.

After Piñero's appointment, members of Congress revisited some of the ideas Truman had proposed earlier. Although lawmakers did not organize a plebiscite, they did pass the Crawford-Butler Act, which allows for Puerto Ricans to elect their own governor rather than have one appointed by the president. This legislation, signed into law by Truman in 1947, was a step toward greater self-rule for the island.

Operation Bootstrap

Puerto Ricans got their first chance to vote for governor in 1948, and Luis Muñoz Marín won the election. Soon after taking office, he began a program referred to as Operation Bootstrap. The program's goal was to kick-start the island's weak economy by offering tax breaks, loans, free land, factory buildings, and the manpower of thousands of unemployed Puerto Rican workers to American companies that were willing to bring jobs to the island.

During the postwar years, America's economy was booming and many companies took advantage of the benefits offered by Operation Bootstrap. The program enjoyed widespread success early on. Kal Wagenheim and Olga Jiménez de Wagenheim, who have written extensively about Puerto Rico, describe the radical changes that took place on the island under Operation Bootstrap:

A poor, rural island transformed itself into a "semideveloped" society; fac-

tories replaced farms as the chief means to earn a living; schools and medical care were made available to virtually all citizens, a large middle class emerged, cars clogged new cement highways, and thousands of tourists streamed in each year, to bask in the Caribbean sun. [19]

A Safety Valve

Operation Bootstrap succeeded in attracting American companies to the island and improving the standard of living. However, not everyone who needed work could find a job in a new factory. To make matters worse, farming, which had traditionally been the backbone of the island's economy, declined during this period.

The large number of unemployed workers was attributed, at least in part, to overpopulation on the island. Believing that island businesses could not generate enough jobs to employ the growing population, Puerto Rican officials began to discuss encouraging migration as an option for some unemployed workers. It would act as a safety valve, reducing competition for jobs among those who stayed on the island. At the same time, it would allow those jobless Puerto Ricans who chose to migrate to take advantage of new opportunities in the United States, as well as in other countries such as Brazil and the Dominican Republic.

As a result of these discussions, Puerto Rico's government created the Bureau of Employment and Migration. Although it was unusual for a government agency to encourage or discourage migration, Clarence Senior, the director of the bureau's

A Puerto Rican worker manufactures automobile parts in a factory in San Juan. Under Operation Bootstrap, American companies opened several factories in Puerto Rico.

New York office, believed that under the circumstances an exception could be made:

> [The Bureau of Employment and Migration] realizes that until the island's economic development has reached a point where it can offer job opportunities and economic security to its workers, ambitious citizens, who can, will search elsewhere. Therefore, the Government strives to help those who decide to leave to adjust more quickly in their new home community. [20]

To help those who chose to migrate, the bureau offered a number of aids. It main-tained offices in American cities, for example, in an effort to stay current with new job openings. The bureau also distributed publications that prepared Puerto Ricans for what they might encounter in their move to the United States. The publications touched on a variety of topics ranging from racial prejudice to the U.S. climate.

Contract Laborers

In addition to its other duties, the bureau operated a program for contract laborers. The program arranged for Puerto Ricans to travel to the United States, where they worked on farms during seasonal harvests.

Among their many assignments, contract laborers harvested peaches in South Carolina, sugar beets in Michigan, potatoes in New Jersey, and tomatoes in Pennsylvania.

To recruit workers for this program, the island's government conducted a widespread campaign in rural areas. The Farm Placement Division, which was part of the island's Department of Labor, promoted "Opportunity for Agricultural Workers in the United States" through advertisements on radio programs, and in newspapers, posters, and flyers.[21] The ads promised fair wages and an eight-hour workday.

Farmhands who were interested in the program registered at their local employment office. Eligibility requirements included a certificate of good health, a birth certificate, letters of recommendation, and identification photographs. Once approved, the laborers signed a contract with a representative of their new employer and traveled to the United States to begin work.

When the harvests were done and their contracts were over, many farmhands returned to the island. Some, however, chose to settle in the United States permanently. They often settled in the areas where they had received contract work. In this way, the contract laborers established a growing number of Puerto Rican communities outside of New York City.

Although the farmhands were all male, Puerto Rican women were also eligible for contract work as maids. Young, single Puerto Rican women could receive contracts to work as domestics in the United States, which was experiencing a shortage of household workers. Private and government agencies orchestrated these contract programs, which transported hundreds of domestics to Illinois, Pennsylvania, New Jersey, and New York.

The Commonwealth of Puerto Rico

As Puerto Rican farmhands and maids received contracts to work in the United States, the island's government was transforming yet again. The status debate, which

Puerto Rican nationalist Oscár Collazo was initially sentenced to death after his failed attempt to assassinate President Harry S. Truman in 1950.

had never been settled to the satisfaction of many Puerto Ricans, took a new turn in 1950. That July, Congress passed Public Law 600. It permitted Puerto Ricans to write their own constitution and base the island's government upon it. Though it granted neither independence nor statehood, Public Law 600 did provide an opportunity for much greater self-rule than ever before.

Not everyone on the island was happy with Public Law 600, however. Some nationalists still hoped for complete independence for their island. When they saw that hope start to fade, they resorted to violence. On October 30, 1950, five nationalists attacked the governor's mansion in San Juan. Uprisings in other towns caused twenty-seven deaths. Then, just a few days later, two Puerto Rican nationalists attempted the boldest assault to date. Griselio Torresola and Oscár Collazo tried, without success, to assassinate President Truman in Washington.

Despite the opposition of radical nationalists, Public Law 600 moved forward. To begin the process, Puerto Ricans elected ninety-two delegates to a constitutional convention. The delegates met from September 1951 to February 1952. While they worked on the constitution, the delegates also drafted two resolutions. Resolution 22 gave a name to the island's new government. It stated, "The body politic created by our Constitution shall be designated 'The Commonwealth of Puerto Rico' in English and 'El Estado Libre Asociado de Puerto Rico' in Spanish."[22] Resolution 23 affirmed that after passing the constitution, "we attain the goal of complete self-government, the last vestiges of colonialism having disappeared."[23]

The delegates approved both of the resolutions as well as the constitution in February 1952. That March, Puerto Ricans were granted the opportunity to vote on the constitution, and they overwhelmingly approved it. Members of Congress also approved the document, and so, on July 25, 1952, Governor Muñoz Marín officially declared the establishment of the Commonwealth of Puerto Rico. The whole process had been a compromise. The United States had retained control over a valuable asset in the Caribbean, while the islanders had gained greater sovereignty.

The Leapfrog Effect

While Puerto Rico's government had made progress, its economy was still weak and a great many people were unemployed. The lure of jobs continued to draw migrants to the mainland. Migration reached its peak in 1953, when 74,603 Puerto Ricans settled on the mainland.

As migration reached new heights, so, too, did the number of letters migrants sent to relatives back on the island. They would enthusiastically describe how much more money workers could make on the mainland compared to the island. And since the cost of living was virtually the same in both places, they could take home much more money at the end of the day. This allowed for new luxuries such as radios, television sets, and washing machines.

The migrants extolled other benefits in their letters as well. One man described these benefits by saying, "Some people thought

A family of Puerto Rican migrants gathers around the table in their tiny Harlem apartment. Many migrants in the United States encouraged family and friends back home to join them.

they could better the lot of their children by coming here, even if they couldn't better their own. . . . You have good unions in New York. You have health benefits. You have old-age pensions. You have social security."[24]

The letters had quite an impact, and they directly contributed to additional Puerto Rican settlements on the mainland. The Migration Division, formerly the Bureau of Employment and Migration, arranged for thirty-six Puerto Rican men to settle in Milwaukee, Wisconsin, and work at an iron foundry in the mid-1950s. As each man succeeded, he sent a letter and perhaps some money to friends or relatives on the island and encouraged them to move to the mainland. Based on the letters these migrants sent home, in just a few years this small group of men multiplied into a community of more than three thousand migrants.

Likewise, in Haverstraw, New York, one Puerto Rican migrant arrived to work as a mechanic. He was successful and wrote to his brother, who arrived shortly afterward. The brothers wrote to more family members, friends, and neighbors, and the efforts snowballed. Within a few short years, Haverstraw and its neighboring areas had a Puerto Rican community of more than nine hundred residents, all from the same island town. This phenomenon has popularly been called the Leapfrog Effect.

The Air Bridge

The migrants who settled in Milwaukee, Haverstraw, and other parts of the country had a much different way of traveling to the mainland than their predecessors. Airplanes had begun to replace steamships as the main means of transportation to U.S. shores during the postwar years. Close to thirty airlines began offering flights from San Juan's airport, with regular service to the United States. Travel by airplane gained such popularity among Puerto Ricans that the route connecting San Juan and New York was nicknamed the air bridge.

Air travel held many advantages for Puerto Ricans. Fares were reasonably priced, usually costing less than $75 per ticket. Air travel was also fast. The first airborne migrants traveled on two-engine planes that made the sixteen-hundred-mile trip from San Juan to New York in about eight hours. This was a vast improvement over steamships, which took four days or longer to travel the same distance. Air-planes were also readily available, and they could transport far more passengers in a week's time than the slow-moving steamers. This streamlined system of transporting migrants led Peter Kihss, a journalist for the New York Times, to dub a plane traveling from San Juan to the mainland the "modern Mayflower."[25]

This was the first time many migrants had ever flown on an airplane, and the journey made quite an impression upon them. A migrant named Toña recalls her journey to the mainland:

I remember the trip as if it were yesterday, and it was seventeen years ago. Luisa, my sister, gave me a shopping

Identification Cards

When Puerto Rican migrants landed in the United States, they received identification cards that were issued by the Puerto Rican government. Each card contained a migrant's photograph and fingerprints, as well as facts including the migrant's physical description, birth date, birthplace, occupation, and address. Many migrants used these cards to prove that they were U.S. citizens, which helped them secure jobs. The identification cards, which were issued until the 1990s, have today become a valuable resource for Puerto Ricans seeking to learn more about their ancestors who migrated to the mainland years ago.

bag filled with sandwiches, coffee, and beer. I came with a friend of mine called Monica. She was used to traveling and was very happy, but it was the first time that I had gone anywhere in a plane. I don't even want to remember the trip! It cost me $45. My son went free because he was an infant.

It was about seven in the evening when I got into that apparatus. I came by Pan American and the stewardess was a very nice little American girl named Nora. Right away they gave me another seat so that the baby could sleep and they brought me something to eat. But I wouldn't even for the sake of God! I kept smelling a lemon so I wouldn't vomit. . . .

The plane carried eighty-five passengers, most of them migrants who were coming to work in the fields of Miami. Those *jíbaros* [peasant farmers] began to vomit and I helped the stewardess give them paper bags. Not even God could have stood the smell in that plane.[26]

Although the conditions on the flights were not always pleasant, airplanes had rev-

Air travel revolutionized Puerto Rican migration, enabling more migrants to come to the United States. Here, a large Puerto Rican family poses after arriving in Miami.

olutionized Puerto Rican migration. The ease and affordability of traveling by plane, coupled with the island's lack of jobs and family members who were already established on the mainland, encouraged thousands of Puerto Ricans to travel to the United States. As a result, Puerto Ricans became the first large-scale group of migrants to arrive in the United States by plane rather than steamship.

First Impressions

Once their planes landed at American airports, many Puerto Ricans were discouraged by their first impressions of their new homeland. According to one migrant, "The truth is that I was disillusioned when I saw New York because I thought it would be a cleaner and prettier place and that the houses would be newer. I was disappointed to see so many slums. I thought, 'Puerto Rico is much prettier than this!'"[27]

Other migrants who arrived in the winter months remember the shock and discomfort brought on by the cold, blustery weather that greeted them. One migrant named José describes this experience:

When I arrived I wanted to turn around and go right back to Puerto Rico because it was so cold. I came in January . . . and there had been a tremendous snowstorm. There were about seven inches of snow on the ground and it was below zero. I said to myself, "Mmmm, I'm not liking this country very much." But then I told myself, "Go on, get off the plane. Let's see what it's like."[28]

Despite the cold weather and slums, the Puerto Ricans who arrived during the period of the Great Migration clung to their hopes of finding new opportunities. Many sought advice from their friends, relatives, and former neighbors who were established in the United States to help them meet the challenges of getting settled.

Making Ends Meet

One of the first challenges migrants faced was getting a job. While some Puerto Ricans had secured contract work before they left the island, others were faced with the task of starting from scratch once they arrived on American soil. The few trained professionals were able to find jobs in their fields. However, as in the past, a majority of migrants were unskilled. So they often took factory jobs such as cutting and packing meat or working on assembly lines. Others found work in the service industry as dishwashers, busboys, or porters.

To find these jobs, many men relied on their network of friends and relatives living on the mainland. One Puerto Rican migrant describes how this process worked:

The friends meet them at Idlewild [now John F. Kennedy International Airport] and take them in to live with them. The next thing is to find a job, and a friend can help there, too. He will take the new man to the factory or wherever else he's working. That's the first approach, and if it doesn't succeed he'll try something else. In general he will know which factories are taking on help. For instance, in

A Garment Worker's Story

By the 1950s New York's garment industry employed approximately twenty thousand Puerto Rican women. This type of work was a natural fit for many Puerto Rican girls and women, because they had experience with this industry on the island. In an interview with the *Magazine of History,* Lucila Padrón recalls: "I was born in Ponce, Puerto Rico. That's where I was raised and went to school. I started doing needlework when I was a little girl, in order to help my parents, because we were poor. After the housework and school, instead of playing, we had to sew. It was a sacrifice."

Padrón and her sisters worked from home. The girls embroidered and sewed the garments by hand for rock-bottom wages. Then the garments were shipped to New York and sold in expensive department stores such as Wanamaker's.

When Padrón moved to the United States in 1927, she was shocked by this disparity between her wages and the selling price of the finished garment. "When I came to New York, I saw the clothes we made selling in Wanamaker's on 14th Street," says Padrón. "Here, those robes or dresses sold for $100 or more. There, they used to pay us for one of those dresses, with all that embroidery—three dollars. So, to earn ten or twelve dollars a week, we had to work day and night."

Once she arrived in New York, Padrón had hoped to stop sewing and instead focus on her schoolwork. However, she had to continue working in the garment industry to help her family make ends meet. "I worked in garment factories for 30 years, working so I could get where I am now and give my children an education. And I'm very proud of that."

parts of the summer, the garment industry is busy on fall and winter wear. Then in the fall the toy factories are going great guns, and the makers of jewelry and novelties. There are lots of others too, and with any luck he should get a job soon.[29]

While their husbands searched for jobs, some Puerto Rican women maintained their traditional roles of keeping the home and raising children. However, many women also earned wages to help their families make ends meet. Some women, like their husbands and brothers, took jobs at factories where they worked on assembly lines. The garment industry also provided many jobs, and Puerto Rican women often found work as sewing machine operators. Rather than sewing an entire piece of clothing from start to finish, however, they worked on specific sections of each garment. It was not uncommon, for example, for a Puerto Rican worker to spend an entire day sewing zippers into dresses or collars onto shirts.

Puerto Rican women caring for their small children were less likely to want factory work. Rather, they often tried to earn money by providing child care services in their homes or renting rooms to lodgers.

Thousands of women also earned money from home by taking in piecework. This involved receiving a "lot" from a manufacturer who, in turn, paid a woman for each piece of the lot that she completed. Hemming handkerchiefs, decorating lampshades, making blouse collars, or embroidering garments were typical piecework assignments. Piecework did not pay well. But according to Doña Clara Rodríguez, a

Most unskilled Puerto Ricans found work in factories or on assembly lines. Here, a group of mostly women assembles radios.

young mother who worked with her sister-in-law to hem twenty dozen handkerchiefs a day, "You'd be surprised how that extra money helped us to buy little extras—or helped to stretch my husband's earnings."[30]

Easing the Transition

Puerto Ricans worked hard to support their families, but they were treated as foreigners in the United States. Many spoke English poorly or not at all, and their culture and customs differed from those of mainstream America. As a result, migrants faced a long and trying period of becoming accustomed to life as Puerto Ricans in the United States.

To ease this transition, many Puerto Ricans formed clubs. More than two hundred of these clubs were prospering in America by the early 1950s. In New York City, hometown clubs were the most common kind. Each club's members gathered for social events, such as celebrating their hometown's feast day. The clubs were more than just social groups, however. They also provided aid for those members who needed help finding jobs or housing, and they helped maintain ties with the island as well.

Yet even with the help of the social clubs in easing the transition from island to mainland culture, many migrants were more comfortable when they could navigate the city using their own language. Spanish-language newspapers, such as *La Prensa, El Imparcial,* and *El Diario,* allowed migrants to stay abreast of local and international events as well as news directly from Puerto Rico. Beyond that, by the 1950s the city had approximately thirty movie theaters that showed films in Spanish. The films were imported from Spain, Argentina, and Mexico. Every day, scores of migrants arrived at the theaters to see the latest Western, musical, or gangster film.

Although many migrants preferred to speak Spanish, some thought their children would have an easier time adjusting to life in the mainland if they spoke more English. Teódula Pérez, who arrived in the United States just before her eleventh birthday, remembers that almost from the moment her family arrived in their Brooklyn apartment, her father told the children, "You are now in the United States of America, of which we are part, and you are to speak English. I want to hear English."[31]

Growing up in the United States with a father who wanted to hear her speak English did not mean that Pérez was divorced from the island's culture. She, and thousands of other migrant children like her, lived in homes where Puerto Rican culture reigned. They listened to Puerto Rican music and learned to dance the *pachanga* and the *merengue.* And when sitting down to a meal, they commonly ate Puerto Rican dishes such as *asopao,* a hearty stew made of meat or fish, or *arroz con habichuelas,* Puerto Rican–style rice and beans.

Nationalists Attack Congress

That the majority of Puerto Rican migrants established themselves in their new homeland peaceably is inarguable. A few, however, settled in the United States with less noble intentions. Puerto Rican nationalists were still irate that Puerto Rico was not independent. Despite the fact that the island

La Marqueta

Amid the many immigrant groups living in Manhattan, Puerto Ricans established their own areas of influence. One of these was La Marqueta. It was a busy marketplace in East Harlem where more than five hundred vendors sold everything from traditional Puerto Rican salt fish to hair ribbons. When *Newsday* profiled the efforts to refurbish La Marqueta in a 2003 article, Marta Moreno Vega, who grew up in East Harlem during the years of the Great Migration, was happy to share her memories. According to Vega, La Marqueta was a place where "there were all these stalls and they were next to each other. It was a place where you would spend the whole day. Just as in the markets in Latin America, it was a thread that tied the community together."

A couple buys produce at East Harlem's La Marqueta, where vendors sold many different traditional Puerto Rican goods.

had been a commonwealth of the United States since 1952, the nationalists refused to give up their cause, and once again a small team of radicals led another round of violence.

On March 1, 1954, four nationalists arrived at the gallery of the U.S. House of Representatives, and at approximately 2:30 P.M. they opened fire on the floor of the House chamber. At first, representatives thought the pistol shots were firecrackers. By the time they realized that the noise they heard was in fact gunfire, they heard the shooters scream, "Viva Puerto Rico!" Lolita Lebrón, considered the leader of the group, then threw down her pistol, unfurled a Puerto Rican flag, and began waving it in the air as five members of the House of Representatives lay bleeding.

The nationalists' goal had been to humiliate the United States at the Inter-American Conference, which had begun in Caracas, Venezuela, on that day. After the nationalists were arrested, the police found a note in Lebrón's purse that seemed to sum up the entire episode: "Before God and the world my blood claims for the independence of Puerto Rico. My life I give for the freedom of my country. This is a cry for a victory in our struggle for independence. Which for more than half a century has tried to conquer that land that belongs to Puerto Rico." [32]

Many migrants were outraged by the acts of violence the nationalists had committed, and quickly condemned the shootings. "The nationalists are not representative of our native country," said one migrant. "We are proud to be citizens." [33]

CHAPTER THREE

The "Puerto Rican Problem"

Not surprisingly, the years of Puerto Rico's Great Migration had a tremendous impact on the communities where the migrants had settled: cities in Illinois, Pennsylvania, Connecticut, Ohio, and New Jersey, but mainly in New York. Since more than 90 percent of Puerto Rican migrants looking for job opportunities chose the Big Apple, that is where the greatest impact of their migration was felt. By 1953 one in twenty New Yorkers was of Puerto Rican descent.

As the face of the city changed to reflect its newest inhabitants, longtime residents began to cast a suspicious eye on Puerto Ricans. They blamed Puerto Rican street gangs for the city's juvenile delinquency and accused migrants of settling on the mainland for the sake of claiming welfare checks. They resented the strain that the thousands of Puerto Rican children put on the city's public schools and grew impatient with many migrants' lack of English skills. Eventually, these frustrations evolved into what longtime New York residents began referring to as the "Puerto Rican problem."

The Language Barrier

In the winter of 1953, when the idea that a "Puerto Rican problem" existed was picking up momentum, the *New York Times* ran

"With an Hispano It's Different"

Anthropologist Oscar Lewis made it his mission to "give a voice to the people who are rarely heard." During the years of the "Puerto Rican problem," this took Lewis to New York City's Puerto Rican neighborhoods. There, he tape-recorded a number of interviews with Puerto Rican migrants on everything from their first impressions of the city to police brutality. Demetrio, whom Lewis interviewed for his book Study of Slum Culture: Backgrounds for La Vida, *spoke candidly about the harsh realities of the language barrier in the workplace.*

Hispanos are the only ones in New York who have to work for practically nothing. The colored people are a bit better off than the Hispanos because at least they know English. . . . A colored man gets a job in a factory and the boss explains clearly to him what he is supposed to do. But suppose he's working at something and the boss says, "Look, hand me that piece of paper." He'll tell the boss, "Pick it up yourself," and go on with what he is doing. With an Hispano it's different. . . .

What else can he do? He doesn't know the language and if he quits the job he will have a hard time finding another one. All because he doesn't know English. That's what keeps us down. In a factory we have to do all the odd jobs because we don't have the advantage of speaking English.

a series of articles dissecting the issue. According to the series' author, Peter Kihss, "The Puerto Ricans' most difficult employment and adjustment problem is a lack of knowledge of English."[34]

Although English had joined Spanish as an official language of the island in 1902, many Puerto Rican migrants lacked fluency in English when they arrived on the mainland. This was blamed partially on Puerto Rican teachers who had not mastered the English language. However, there was something else at play as well—many Puerto Ricans were reluctant to give up their native tongue, which had been spoken on the island for more than four hundred years.

The lack of English fluency set up barriers for the new migrants. Parents could not easily communicate with their children's English-speaking teachers. Job applicants struggled to articulate their skills and experiences during interviews. Patients had a hard time describing their symptoms to doctors. Those seeking aid from government programs, such as welfare or public housing, were in trouble if they had to communicate with a clerk who spoke only English.

To overcome the language barriers, some Puerto Ricans enrolled in English classes. The New York City Department of Welfare, for example, offered a course that taught 550 basic English words. Many other Puerto Ricans relied upon their children for help with the English language. Esmeralda Santiago, who arrived in the United States in 1961 at the age of thirteen, remembers having to translate her mother's request to receive welfare benefits:

> When Mami was laid off, we had to go on welfare. She took me with her because she needed someone to translate. Six months after we landed in Brooklyn, I spoke enough English to explain our situation.
>
> "My mother she no spik inglish. My mother she look for work evree day, and nothing. My mother she say she don't want her children suffer. My mother say she want work bot she lay off. My mother she only need help a leetle while."
>
> I was always afraid that if I said something wrong, if I mispronounced a word or used the wrong tense, the social workers would say no, and we might be evicted from our apartment, or the electricity would be shut off, or we'd freeze to death because Mami couldn't pay for the heating fuel.[35]

"Shall I Call You John?"

Santiago was not the only young migrant who had to work to learn English upon arriving in the United States. Nearly 47,000 Puerto Rican students enrolled in public elementary schools in New York City in 1952 alone. Of those students, approximately 40 percent—17,954 students total—came speaking little or no English. As a result, they were often forced to repeat a grade or were placed in low-level classes.

The teachers in New York City's public schools were also overwhelmed. Few had any training in the Spanish language,

This photo pictures Hispanic and African American students at a Harlem elementary school in the 1940s. Most Puerto Rican American students had a limited knowledge of English.

an obvious obstacle to imparting basic skills such as reading, writing, or math. "It is when the Puerto Ricans get to be about 25 to 30 percent of the class," said one school administrator in the late 1950s, "that a real problem is created. Then the teacher must control two separate groups, one of which she can barely communicate with." [36]

The teachers' divided attention led many non–Puerto Rican parents to develop the suspicion that their children were being lost in a flood of new Puerto Rican students, rather than receiving a proper education. With this in mind, many of these parents transferred their children from public schools to private ones.

The public schools, however, could not shut down while administrators decided how to address the challenges. Spanish-speaking aides, called substitute auxiliary teachers, were hired to serve as liaisons between students, parents, and teachers in schools with large Puerto Rican populations. Some schools used a buddy system, pairing recently arrived migrants with ones who were more established. Other schools offered special orientation classes to acquaint students with the English language and life in the city.

The vast majority of teachers, however, simply confronted the language barrier head-on in their classrooms. In an effort to seize control of a trying situation, many teachers took it upon themselves to nudge their young migrant students to become Americanized as quickly as possible. Juan González, who was a student in New York City during the 1950s, describes his experiences in a public school:

"Your name isn't Juan," the young teacher told me in first grade at P.S. 87 in East Harlem. "In this country, it's John. Shall I call you John?" Confused and afraid, but sensing this as some fateful decision, I timidly said no. But most children could not summon the courage, so school officials routinely anglicized their names. Though I had spoken only Spanish before I entered kindergarten, the teachers were amazed at how quickly I mastered English. From then on, each time a new child from Puerto Rico was placed in any of my classes, the teachers would sit him beside me so I could interpret the lessons. Bewildered, terrified, and ashamed, the new kids grappled with my clumsy attempts to decipher the teacher's strange words. [37]

Making the Scene

The process of coping with new schools, learning a new language, and becoming acquainted with a whole new city was challenging for migrants. So throughout the 1950s, a small but highly visible number of young Puerto Ricans formed gangs as a means to make fitting in easier. The gangs offered friendship and a sense of belonging that the young migrants did not find anywhere else in their new homeland.

To identify themselves as members of a particular gang, the young men wore special jackets. They were usually cloth and had small stars made of nickel on the shoulders. The color of a jacket, as well as the name emblazoned on the back of it, sym-

On the Move

The flood of Puerto Rican students into the New York City school system and the language barrier that accompanied it made fitting into a new school difficult for young migrants. However, they also faced another problem: frequent moves. It was not uncommon for migrant families, searching for better living quarters or less expensive rent, to move from one apartment to another every few months. This made it difficult for children to become established in one school.

Statistics from Manhattan's Public School (PS) 108 show how dramatic this rate of moving was when it came to student turnover. In 1952 PS 108 had 1,500 students enrolled, and more than 98 percent of them were Puerto Rican. That year, 674 new students began attending the school and another 432 transferred to other schools. That means out of the total student body of 1,500 children in PS 108, more than 1,106 students had changed schools in just one year. Because of the frequent moves, they constantly had to make new friends and get used to a new teacher, as well as learn English and become accustomed to life in a strange new country.

bolized membership in a specific gang. According to a priest who worked in one of New York City's Puerto Rican neighborhoods, "The gangs might even go out of existence if their members couldn't buy those jackets in special colors."[38]

Gang members often enjoyed harmless activities such as stickball, picnics, and dances. Gang life also had a darker side, however, and many members used or sold drugs. Members also carried knives and pistols, which were brought out during street fights with Italian, Irish, and African American gangs. The fights frequently resulted in arrests and injuries. Each incident created a burning desire for vengeance, which fueled future street fights.

Despite its dangers, this lifestyle held tremendous appeal to some newcomers. Gang violence among teenagers was nearly unheard of in Puerto Rico at this time, and so it was generally considered an American experience. As a result, those who partook in this lifestyle believed they showed proof of being legitimate Americans. According to one migrant, "The Puerto Rican kid wants to 'make it' here, but they laugh at him and call him 'greenhorn,' so he shoots dope or starts bopping [fighting] and then he's an American. That's how he makes the scene."[39]

The criminal aspects of gang life drew the attention of New York's media, with newspaper headlines describing the latest violent acts. Although the gangs received a lot of publicity, for the most part the illegal activity was the work of a small percentage of young people. Puerto Rican leaders, weary of having the mainstream press presenting Puerto Ricans as thugs,

Teenage Puerto Rican gang members Salvador Agrón and Antonio Hernández were convicted of killing two white youths in New York in 1959.

took action in 1959. That year, they placed full-page ads in all of New York City's newspapers with a headline that read: "We Too Fight Delinquency." [40] The ad then pointed out that the percentage of crimes committed by Puerto Ricans was equal to, not higher than, the percentage of Puerto Ricans living in the city. It also reminded readers that the majority of Puerto Ricans contributed to society by earning an honest living and paying more than $90 million in taxes each year.

A Housing Shortage

As Puerto Ricans fought for respect in the newspapers, they also faced another diffi-

culty. During the 1950s New York experienced a housing shortage. This came at the same time that Puerto Rican migration was at its height, and many New Yorkers concluded that the housing shortage had been caused by the influx of migrants. In truth, however, the shortage of housing, especially decent housing for families with low incomes, had begun decades earlier, when the Great Depression had nearly put an end to the construction of new homes and apartment buildings. Like other New Yorkers, Puerto Ricans suffered from the housing shortage, and many found themselves living in crowded, aging tenements.

According to Charles Abrams, New York State's rent administrator during the 1950s, the conditions were deplorable. In 1955, after touring some of the tenements, Abrams described the conditions he found:

> In [East] Harlem I saw a six-story, 25-foot-wide tenement on East 100th Street in which 170 Puerto Ricans were living. . . . 12 people were living in one three-room apartment. Every hall window was broken. Splintered stair treads sank perilously with each step. Almost every toilet was out of order. Plaster hung from the hall ceilings; great heaps of garbage rotted under the stairways; a dead rat was on the landing. [41]

Migrants had to put up with other unhealthy conditions as well. Cockroaches and bedbugs infested apartments, and it was not uncommon for small children to be bitten by rats while asleep in their beds. In the winter residents stuffed newspapers into cracks around window frames to keep out the bitter wind. Despite the terrible conditions, tenement landlords charged Puerto Ricans high rents, and by ignoring necessary repairs they were able to turn large profits. Many of the city's more conscientious landlords were leery of the risk involved in renting to new migrants, which allowed the slumlords to raise their rents with little competition.

Even with the trying conditions, many Puerto Ricans managed to make their apartments cozy. Families hung curtains, displayed photographs, painted the walls in bright colors, and placed religious icons of Jesus and the Virgin Mary throughout their homes. Smells from traditional Puerto Rican dishes wafted through the air, and programs from radios and televisions brought daily entertainment into many apartments.

The Welfare Rolls

The housing crisis, gang violence, and overburdened schools were not the only issues the New Yorkers considered to be part of the "Puerto Rican problem." At the heart of the matter was public aid. During the 1950s New Yorkers routinely accused Puerto Ricans of moving to the mainland solely to receive welfare benefits. As the number of Puerto Ricans on welfare rolls grew, so did anger and resentment toward the newcomers.

These accusations were further inflamed by rumors surrounding shady deals by Vito Marcantonio, a U.S. representative from New York whose constituents included many Puerto Ricans. Critics accused Marcantonio of paying for migrants to journey to the United States in exchange for their votes. Once the migrants arrived, Marcantonio would allegedly exert his power as a representative to get the newcomers on the welfare rolls. Then he would take a cut from the relief given to the migrants and use that money to bankroll the passage of more migrants to the mainland, thus ensuring he received more votes and would win his next election.

While the rumors of Marcantonio's scheme were never proven, they served to create a rift between the established residents of New York and the newcomers. In truth, however, migrants did not receive as much aid as concerned New Yorkers suggested. According to New York City's welfare commissioner, Henry L. McCarthy, approximately one out of fourteen Puerto Rican migrants actually received public assistance in the early 1950s. Those who did receive assistance typically needed it for much less time than non–Puerto Ricans.

In an effort to expose this issue, the *New York Times* profiled a typical Puerto Rican migrant's experience on public assistance. The twenty-six-year-old man profiled arrived in New York in 1951 and found a job earning $33 a week delivering orders for a delicatessen. A year later, he sent for his wife and three small children. The additional expense of feeding, clothing, and housing four more family members required him to apply for aid with the Welfare Department. His request was soon granted, along with information about a better-paying job opportunity. He received the job and soon earned a raise so he was making $45 a week. This allowed him to go off welfare in less than four months' time.

U.S. representative Vito Marcantonio was accused of paying for Puerto Rican migrants to come to the United States in exchange for political support.

The dilapidated tenement buildings seen in this 1947 photo of kids at play in Harlem give some idea of the crowded, squalid conditions in which most migrants lived.

At the Doctor's Office

Some mainstream Americans suspected Puerto Ricans also migrated to the United States to take advantage of free medical care. At this time, the United States had a number of free clinics and hospitals that served poor, uninsured patients who could not afford treatment elsewhere. Some New Yorkers believed that Puerto Ricans arrived in New York City with the sole purpose of seeking treatment at these free facilities and then, upon their recovery, immediately returning to the island. Critics argued that these migrants had no intention of permanently settling in the United States, getting jobs, paying taxes, and contributing to the city that had provided them with the benefits.

Taking advantage of free medical care was just one medical-related concern surrounding Puerto Rican migrants. Doctors also believed that some Puerto Ricans arrived in the United States carrying illnesses such as tuberculosis, a contagious disease that affects the lungs. Some doctors recommended having migrants undergo chest X-rays before they left the island to prove they did not have tuberculosis. However, as U.S. citizens Puerto Ricans were not subject to federal immigration laws that required medical examinations before entering the country. To force Puerto Ricans to have these exams, many argued, would be a violation of the Fourth Amendment right to security from "unreasonable searches and seizures."

Doctors worried also about health conditions specific to Puerto Ricans. They believed the traditional Puerto Rican diet had too few green vegetables and too much white rice, increasing a migrant's chances of malnutrition and disease. Doctors were also concerned about such unsanitary, disease-producing conditions as garbage bags stored in rooms and hallways. City officials issued flyers in Spanish and English on the importance of proper sanitation and good nutrition, but often these materials were disregarded as nothing more than red tape.

A Nation of Red Tape

As Puerto Ricans entered the American mainstream, they often found themselves stymied by bureaucratic requirements and paperwork known collectively as red tape. Government agencies, for example, often asked the migrants to fill out forms that seemed bizarre and, in some cases, irrelevant. A social worker who regularly met with Puerto Rican migrants in the late 1950s describes this problem:

> They ask a man all kinds of crazy things. To list all the assets he owns— or has ever owned. To list everything he derives income from—or has ever derived income from. Questions like that are meaningless when a man has never owned anything but a hut he built himself from old boards. He finds that as he answers the questions he gets deeper and deeper into trouble, so he learns to dummy up and not tell the whole story. Of course that's likely to hurt him, really—to ruin his

chances, say, of getting into a housing project. [42]

Often, basic cultural differences produced the greatest misunderstandings. For example, Puerto Ricans follow the Spanish tradition of having two last names, one from the father and one from the mother. So a student named Guillermo López Moreno, for instance, might be listed as Guillermo López in some school records and as Guillermo Moreno in others. This cultural misunderstanding caused considerable confusion in schools as well as government offices, especially if the clerks filing the records were unfamiliar with Spanish naming customs.

Discrimination

Part of the fallout from the "Puerto Rican problem" was the discrimination migrants faced every day. Puerto Ricans found that they were often passed over for promotions, labeled as slum dwellers, and considered backward and unsophisticated.

Some Americans also offended Puerto Ricans by calling them "spics." The origin of this term was explained to migrant Esmeralda Santiago by her father, who said, "There are many Puerto Ricans in New York, and when someone asks them a question, they say, 'I don spik inglish' instead of 'I don't speak English.' They make fun of our accent." [43]

Such prejudices were not limited to New York. Other communities where Puerto Ricans settled suffered from the same tensions, which frequently involved skin color. In Spring Garden, a predominantly white neighborhood of Philadelphia, a migrant recalled that "when I went there [Spring Garden] to look for apartments, they throw the door in my face. They don't want no colored people, you know, my skin is dark." [44] The long-simmering tensions erupted at a bar in Spring Garden in July 1953, sparking riots that stretched across two blocks and involved between three hundred and one thousand people. The riots, which lasted two hours, further separated the migrants from the established community.

Even Puerto Rican children experienced widespread discrimination. According to Félix Matos Rodríguez, the director of the Center for Puerto Rican Studies at New York City's Hunter College, life was especially difficult for those students who spoke no English. "They were being branded as dummies," Matos Rodríguez says. "They were being branded as sort of unteachable." [45]

Chicago's Model Minority

Frustrated with the conditions in New York, many migrants considered moving, and the city at the top of the list for many families was Chicago. This preference, coupled with newly added direct flights between San Juan and Chicago, brought thousands of Puerto Ricans to the city. Chicago and its suburbs quickly become home to the nation's second-largest Puerto Rican population.

Unlike New York, where the "Puerto Rican problem" still lingered, residents of Chicago generally welcomed and admired the migrants. According to author Maura Toro-Morn, during the 1950s in Chicago "the local press . . . found the Puerto Rican story of hardworking men and strong families a compelling one. For over a decade, local newspapers hailed Puerto Ricans as 'examples of good citizens' and a 'model minority.'" [46]

From Puerto Rican to Hispano

The discrimination Puerto Ricans faced as a result of the "Puerto Rican problem" led many to change how they referred to themselves. Rather than calling themselves Puerto Ricans, some took to saying they were "Hispanos." This left their country of origin ambiguous—under the name Hispano a person could be from any Spanish-speaking country, from Spain to Argentina. This allowed Puerto Ricans to assume a less controversial place in New York society.

In the late 1950s anthropologist Elena Padilla studied this phenomenon in one Puerto Rican community, which she renamed Eastville to protect the anonymity of the people there. "When referring to friends, or to persons considered 'decent and respectable,' the term 'Hispano' is preferred by Eastville Puerto Ricans," writes Padilla in *Up from Puerto Rico*. "Recently arrived migrants soon learn that they are to call themselves Hispanos and drop their identification as Puerto Ricans. They will probably not deny their country, but will resort to . . . Hispano to protect themselves from being characterized in a derogatory manner."

This response was clearly in sharp contrast to the reception Puerto Ricans usually met in New York. Much of the responsibility for this difference lies with Chicago's office of the island's Migration Division. Its leaders promoted the Puerto Ricans as a group to the mainstream community in an effort to prevent conflicts like the ones occurring in New York. It sponsored films such as *The Girl from Puerto Rico* and *The Crowded Island* to foster greater understanding. It also used radio spots and print media to provide information about Puerto Rican migrants, playing up strengths such as a good work ethic and strong family ties.

Indeed, these efforts seemed to have the intended effect. Puerto Ricans living in Chicago, although certainly not completely free from discrimination and other challenges such as poor housing, were better

In 1963 an African American child leads his peers in the flag salute at a Chicago elementary school. The students are of various ethnicities.

received than those living in New York. An article that appeared in Chicago's *Daily Tribune* described the situation:

> Everyone who has seen *West Side Story* or reads the papers or has seen Spanish Harlem in New York knows there is a "Puerto Rican problem."
>
> He can talk knowledgeably about gang fights and knives and five Puerto Ricans hanging themselves in New York jails and all the other problems of the Spanish ghetto.
>
> It has been printed and reprinted that more Puerto Ricans, sick of subway knifings and dirty air and dirty tenements, are going back to Puerto Rico than are coming to New York.
>
> The surprising thing is that none of this is true in Chicago. [47]

In Defense of Puerto Ricans

Meanwhile, in New York Puerto Ricans were not completely alone in their struggles. Many civic leaders recognized the difficulties the migrants faced and worked to help them clear their reputation. Their hope was that if this growing segment of the population was treated more kindly, perhaps some of the finger-pointing would stop and more progress toward improving the migrants' circumstances could begin.

In this vein, Henry L. McCarthy, the city's welfare commissioner, issued a glowing report in 1952. In the report, McCarthy revealed that more than 90 percent of Puerto Ricans had become accustomed to their new life in New York and had found employment. "Their special disadvantages,

New York secretary of state Carmine DeSapio recognized the important role of Puerto Rican migrants in American society.

such as the language barrier and lack of education, hurt their employment opportunities," said McCarthy, "But if the Irish, Germans, and Italians can make it in one generation, the Puerto Ricans can too." [48]

McCarthy wasn't alone in his call to view the Puerto Ricans in a new light. Carmine G. DeSapio, New York's secretary of state, also addressed this issue while speaking at an event hosted by the Caribe Democratic Club in 1955. At the event, the Italian American official publicly condemned the "irresponsible talk about the so-called Puerto Rican problem" and further pressed the issue by saying, "Some of us forget our own parents and grandparents bore the same relationship to their American contemporaries as the Puerto Ricans now bear to us."[49]

Getting Organized

Perhaps inspired by the support given by state leaders such as McCarthy and DeSapio, members of New York's Puerto Rican community began banding together to overcome some of their difficulties. They were tired of the discrimination and they no longer wanted to be viewed as a burden on society. Instead, they wanted to prove they were just as capable as other New Yorkers.

In this cause, Puerto Ricans found a leader in Antonia Pantoja. Pantoja was a teacher from San Juan who had migrated to New York in 1944. She became dismayed by the large number of Puerto Rican stu-

dents who dropped out of high school in the 1950s. So she, along with a handful of other community leaders, founded an organization called Aspira in 1961. Its goal was to provide Puerto Rican students with the resources they needed to complete their education.

Pantoja was not alone in her quest to improve circumstances in the Puerto Rican community. The Migration Division joined with community groups to conduct voter registration drives, which provided thousands of Puerto Ricans with a voice in elections. *El Congreso del Pueblo* (The Council of Hometown Clubs) represented approximately eighty hometown clubs and worked tirelessly to raise awareness of the difficulties mainland Puerto Ricans faced. The Puerto Rican Forum used volunteers and private money to help community organizations thrive. As these efforts were under way, the Revolving-Door Migration was poised to begin.

CHAPTER FOUR

The Revolving Door

The conditions collectively referred to as the "Puerto Rican problem," which surfaced during the years of the Great Migration, caused distress for newcomers and established New York residents alike. Not surprisingly, thousands of Puerto Rican migrants arriving in New York City soon regretted their decision to relocate and began moving back to the island.

However, for a large number of migrants, returning to the island had been their plan all along. They had traveled to the United States with the express intent of staying only for a few years. Their goal was to earn enough money so that they could return to the island and buy a *finca* (small farm), a

new car, or a bigger house. "Tackling New York," says one San Juan resident, "has come to be a sort of initiation, or adventure, that many people here think they should go through. They get prestige from it. It gives them something to talk about when they come home. . . . In a way, it is like going to college." [50]

Indeed, a substantial number of migrants did return to the island of their birth after spending several years on the mainland. Often, however, the lure of high-paying jobs or a desire to be with family members still in the United States would pull them back to the mainland. As time passed, it became common for a Puerto Rican to move

In the 1960s, many Puerto Ricans, like these celebrating a festival in New York, began moving back and forth between the United States and Puerto Rico.

back and forth from one homeland to another. This new back-and-forth lifestyle came to be known as the Revolving-Door Migration. It began in earnest around 1965 and continues today, constituting the third and final wave of Puerto Rican migration.

Reverse Migration Begins

The factors motivating reverse migration did not spring up over night. By the late 1950s an average of ten thousand migrants returned to the island each year. Although many had simply been unhappy on the mainland, others were eager to reap the benefits of Operation Bootstrap, the economic redevelopment program begun by Governor Muñoz Marín that had created many new jobs in Puerto Rico. The return migrants, who had mainland work experience and at least some knowledge of English, had an advantage over islanders when it came to competing for the new positions. Between 1955 and 1960, returning migrants filled 36 percent of the island's new manufacturing and merchant jobs.

As word of the improved economic conditions in Puerto Rico spread among the mainland migrants, the new hope of good jobs on the island caused many to reconsider their decision to live in the United States. They had not come to the mainland seeking refuge or greater freedoms, as other immigrants had. Instead, their main motivation for migration had been finding work. If they could secure good jobs on the island, they would be able to earn a decent living while at the same time escaping the cold weather, discrimination, and slums of New York City. Many began seeing this as a realistic option for improving their lot, and they were anxious to return to the place that they still considered home.

Although tracking the numbers is difficult, since Puerto Ricans may move freely between the island and mainland, by 1964 it appeared that the number of Puerto Ricans returning to the island was

The Migrant Mentality

Because of their strong desire to return to the island as soon as possible, some Puerto Rican migrants were slow to adapt to life on the mainland. They resisted the pressure to assimilate and continued to harbor fantasies about a serene life back on the island. In A Study of Slum Culture: Backgrounds for La Vida, *anthropologist Oscar Lewis writes: "Puerto Ricans were, psychologically speaking, not really immigrants at all, but migrant workers." Domingo, whom Lewis interviewed, sums up this mentality:*

As soon as I can, I want to leave New York with all its "modernization." This "modernization" doesn't go back with me. It's for those who have ability, money, education, and who are on their way up. Perhaps it's for my children in the future but not for me. . . .

When I leave here I'm going to take $800 or $1,000 with me to Puerto Rico. But I'm not going to live like a rich man in the center of San Juan. I'll work in San Juan but I'm going to take my family to live in the countryside, where I can have a little house of my own, even if it's made of planks and has a tin roof. At least I won't have to pay rent. I'll buy a few acres of land and I'll come home and raise my animals and cultivate something. I'll educate my children and perhaps the whole family can live peacefully.

reaching the same level of those who were leaving. In general, the people who chose to return to the island were married couples in their thirties and forties who had children. When they arrived, they established their own communities of return migrants in areas such as Toa Baja, Santa Juanita, and Bayamón.

As their parents searched for jobs, the children of return migrants struggled to fit in. Since most of the children had lived on the mainland their entire lives, this was not easy. Many considered themselves New Yorkers and were unsure how to adapt to their new lives. Rudy Marrero, who returned to the island with his parents at the age of nineteen, described this conflict of identity. According to Marrero, children of return migrants "really don't know what they want or where they belong. They look for kicks here, get tired, go back to New York, and six months later they are back in Puerto Rico."[51]

Return Migrants and the Status Debate

Despite difficulties like those experienced by Marrero, the return migrants continued to stream into Puerto Rico. By the mid-1960s estimates suggested that approximately five hundred thousand of Puerto Rico's 2.3 million residents had spent at least a year living in the United States. As this number grew, Puerto Ricans who had never left the island began noticing differences between themselves and those who had lived in the United States. The return migrants wore American styles of clothing and their Spanish was often peppered with

English words and phrases. And in the political arena, return migrants were strongly against granting independence to the island.

This became an important issue as the tenth anniversary of the commonwealth's founding drew near. In June 1962 Governor Muñoz Marín wrote to President John F. Kennedy in an attempt to clarify the relationship between the island and the main-

Puerto Rican governor Luis Muñoz Marín was instrumental in orchestrating a 1967 plebiscite to vote on the island's relationship with the United States.

land. The eventual outcome of their correspondence was a thirteen-member commission of Puerto Ricans and Americans that convened from 1964 to 1966 to discuss possible options for the island. Commission members listened to testimony from 123 witnesses and wrote a lengthy report, concluding that all three possible options for the island—statehood, independence, and commonwealth—were legitimate and dignified. To determine which of the three paths to follow, commission members recommended allowing Puerto Ricans to vote on the matter in a plebiscite.

In July 1967 the plebiscite took place. The results, perhaps tempered by the influx of return migrants, were overwhelmingly in favor of keeping the island a commonwealth of the United States. More than 60 percent of voters chose the commonwealth status, while 38 percent voted in favor of statehood, and less than 1 percent voted for independence. With this decisive response, Muñoz Marín declared, "The century-old debate about political status has ended."[52]

However, Muñoz Marín's statement was far too optimistic. The status debate, which was so much a part of the Puerto Rican consciousness, would continue to be a hot-button issue for years to come.

The Division Street Riot

Meanwhile, the Puerto Ricans who had chosen to continue living on the mainland faced new struggles. Their adopted homeland was changing, and throughout the late 1960s and early 1970s civil unrest plagued the nation. Riots erupted as minority groups demanded greater civil rights and students protested America's increasing involvement in the Vietnam War. Puerto Rican communities across the United States were not immune to the incendiary atmosphere sweeping the nation at this time, and events that took place in June 1966 made this painfully clear. That summer, the nation's first major Puerto Rican riot broke out in Chicago.

Tensions between Chicago's police officers and Puerto Rican residents had been building for years. Roberto Medina, a Puerto Rican living in the city during this period, explains what form this took in daily life:

> If the police saw you in a car . . . they would pull you out and ask if you were a "wet back" because at that time [every Latino] was a "wet back." . . . They would just pull you out of your cars, totally violate your civil rights, search your car, hit you with their sticks, and just harass you. They would break into our social clubs and stop our activities for no reason whatsoever. It was an ongoing situation with the police—we were not welcome in the city.[53]

Frustrations boiled over on June 12, the day of Chicago's first annual Puerto Rican Day parade. Shortly after the parade ended, a white police officer shot and injured a twenty-year-old Puerto Rican man named Aracelis Cruz, whom officers believed was an armed gang member. As a crowd of angry onlookers gathered, police officers released dogs to disperse them. One of the dogs bit a Puerto Rican, and tensions escalated further.

Witness to the Riot

To commemorate the thirty-first anniversary of the Division Street Riots, writers from the journal Diálogo *interviewed eyewitnesses to the event, who provided snapshots of that difficult time.*

I was able to get to the very center of the riot which at that point was right on the 2000 block of Division, between Hoyne and Damen, when the crowd was accommodating and was growing by the hour. I understood that I was witnessing a social phenomenon. By listening to people, I already sensed the anger against the police. By listening to people I also heard people expressing their grievances.

—Obed López, a Mexican immigrant who worked in the Puerto Rican neighborhood for thirty years

I participated in terms of trying to keep the peace—talking with people, expressing my opinion. . . . Some people thought that it was a bunch of yahoos within the community, criminals that started the whole thing. That wasn't true. It had to do with . . . the frustrations that we as a community were experiencing. So, I participated by trying to articulate the needs of our community and keeping the peace so that people would not get hurt.

—Roberto Medina, an eighteen-year-old Puerto Rican activist

The next day I had to go downtown for something and when I took the bus that day I saw all the damage that had been done to the stores along Division Street. . . . The priests and *reverendos* wanted to group on the street with their collars on, hoping they could calm people down. Unfortunately, that night around five or six o'clock, the riot started again. . . . The religious leaders had asked the police to stay away, instead they [the police] wore riot gear while they patrolled the park. . . . It was a real chaotic situation. It was hard to keep a clear head.

—Mirta Ramírez, founder of Chicago's chapter of Aspira

The area where the shooting had occurred, near the intersection of Division Street and Damen Avenue, quickly became the scene of mass riots. Puerto Ricans looted businesses; smashed windows; burned buildings and squad cars; and threw rocks, bottles, and bricks at police officers. By the time peace was restored to the area three days later, sixteen people had been injured and more than fifty buildings had been destroyed.

The Young Lords

The Division Street Riot had, unquestionably, damaged a Chicago neighborhood and widened the rift between police and the Puerto Rican community. It had also served as a source of inspiration for a group of young Puerto Ricans known collectively as the Young Lords. The Young Lords were a street gang that had begun in Chicago years earlier. After the Division Street Riot, members of the Young Lords wanted to make some real and lasting changes to improve their community. To do this, they looked to the radical Black Panther Party as a role model.

The Black Panthers were militant African Americans who were disillusioned with the slow progress of the civil rights movement. They took it upon themselves to protect their rights through the use of force, as well as through peaceful community projects. Using this as their model, members of the Young Lords transformed their street gang into a community organization. The methods the Young Lords used to achieve their goals, however, were quite controversial.

"The Young Lords' approach was based on the premise that the only significant resource Puerto Ricans possessed was the capacity to make trouble,"[54] said Félix Padilla, a Puerto Rican scholar who frequently writes about Latinos in the United States.

There is no doubt the Young Lords often used forceful and radical tactics. To further their cause, they resorted to vandalism to intimidate white authority figures and even overtook buildings such as churches and schools. However, they also made strides in the community. The Young Lords created day care centers, free breakfast programs, and clothing drives for poor Puerto Rican

Members of the Puerto Rican gang, the Young Lords, pose in front of a van they stole in 1970. The gang employed radical methods to improve living conditions for migrants.

families. They fought for more affordable housing and better basic services, such as garbage collection, in Puerto Rican neighborhoods. Beyond this, they also arranged for medical exams and better clinics for migrants. The group became so successful that new branches were established in other American cities, including New York and Philadelphia.

New Opportunities

While the Young Lords used radical tactics to elicit changes, other Puerto Ricans were looking to improve their communities in different ways. Migrant Miriam Colón, for example, saw a need for the arts to be more accessible to the Puerto Rican community. In 1967 she founded the Puerto Rican Traveling Theatre. It was the first New York theater troupe to perform in Spanish, and its goal was to bring plays to the city's Puerto Rican neighborhoods. It also provided opportunities for Puerto Rican actors and playwrights to demonstrate their craft.

As Colón was making history in theater, a Puerto Rican named Miguel Algarín was making history in another arena. Algarín, a college professor and writer, frequently invited other Puerto Rican artists over to his apart-

Juan González

Juan González was born in Ponce, Puerto Rico, in 1947. Just a year later, his parents, Pepe and Florinda, moved their family to New York. Young Juan grew up in predominantly Puerto Rican neighborhoods, seeing hardship around him every day. While attending Columbia University, González became involved in the civil unrest plaguing the nation. He wanted to draw attention to the plight of Puerto Ricans, so in 1969 he became one of the founding members of the Young Lords.

Faced with difficulties from the FBI and other law enforcement groups, the Young Lords disbanded just a few years after it had started. However, González was not about to give up on his mission. He began working as a journalist and author. Today, his interest in improving

conditions for Puerto Ricans, as well as the rest of the growing Latino population, remains strong.

In a 2001 interview with writer Alex Abella, González reflected on the difficulties of being a Latino when he was young. "When I went to Columbia," said González, "there were no Latino organizations. You could put all the Latinos in one phone booth." González contrasted this with how different the situation is today: "In the next ten years, you're going to see Latinos elected mayors of several major cities in the country, not just Los Angeles and New York, but there's a very big possibility also of Houston, Dallas, and Chicago. You're going to see major runs at the city halls of the major cities because the reality is: that is the growing population at all of these cities."

ment to share their poems, plays, and other writings. These works often concentrated on firsthand experiences of Puerto Ricans living in New York City, which ranged from feelings of isolation from mainstream America to the struggles of growing up in El Barrio. As the number of artists meeting at Algarín's apartment increased, he founded the Nuyorican Poets Café in 1974. It provided a forum where Puerto Ricans, as well as artists of other nationalities, could present their work and allow their creative voices to be heard publicly.

The emerging leaders of the Puerto Rican community effected changes in other segments of their communities as well. Throughout the 1970s many of the changes took place in the world of education. Puerto Rican parents and educators established bilingual education in public schools, with the hope that it would eliminate the sink-or-swim situation earlier migrant children had faced. Puerto Rican leaders were also at work in higher education, and in 1974 the state of New York granted Boricua College permission to begin offering classes. When it opened its doors, it was the nation's first college specifically dedicated to the education of Puerto Rican students. Its emphasis was on presenting materials in a bilingual and bicultural setting, with an emphasis on Puerto Rican heritage.

"I'd Rather Be in My Homeland"

Despite the progress made by Puerto Ricans such as Badillo, Algarín, and bilingual educators, life was growing increasingly difficult for the average Puerto Rican migrant. As the U.S. economy sank into a recession,

Actress Miriam Colón founded the Puerto Rican Traveling Theatre to help make the arts accessible to Puerto Rican migrants.

jobs became harder and harder to find. Manufacturing firms began outsourcing jobs to other countries where labor was cheaper. As factories closed, workers were left jobless. Faced with the inability to support themselves, Puerto Ricans began planning to return to the island. Abelardo Tellado found himself in just that position in 1972 when he was laid off from his job as a metalworker. After six months of unemployment and unable to find any job leads, Tellado decided it was time to return to his roots. "Well, things are bad there, they're bad here—well, all things being equal, I'd rather be in my homeland,"[55] said Tellado.

The metalworker's choice represented a trend. During the 1970s, for the first time in history migrants returning to Puerto Rico outnumbered those leaving for the mainland. In 1972 alone, thirty-four thousand more people returned to Puerto Rico than migrated to the United States. This pattern continued throughout the decade as the economy continued to lag. After interviewing several return migrants, journalist William Stockton concluded that "for the first time in U.S. history, a major immigrant group is giving up on the American dream and returning whence it came." [56]

The return migrants who were making up a growing segment of Puerto Rican society generally fell into one of two groups. The first was made up of those people who had been born on the island and had migrated to the United States as teenagers or young adults to seek jobs. They were native Spanish speakers with a firsthand knowledge of the island, its customs, and its culture. Given their background, they had a fairly easy time slipping back into the society of their childhood when they returned to the island.

The second group of return migrants had a much more difficult time adjusting to island life. These people had been born in the United States to parents who were native Puerto Ricans. They had lived their entire lives on the mainland, spoke English fluently, and in some cases knew of Puerto Rico only through family stories or short vacations. They had never lived on the island, but they moved there throughout the 1970s not only to find a better life but also to rediscover their roots.

These migrants faced more of a challenge fitting into Puerto Rico's society than those who had been raised on the island. Many island residents referred to the American-born return migrants as Nuyoricans or Neoricans. Although these terms fostered a sense of pride and community when used on the mainland, on the island they were used in a derogatory manner. Neoricans living in Puerto Rico were viewed as less "authentic" than Puerto Ricans who had been born on the island. Beyond that, Neoricans, who had American educations and job training, were edging out Puerto Ricans for jobs on the island, where the unemployment rate was a staggering 20 percent. This did little to endear the return migrants to the islanders.

Fitting in on the Island

Also contributing to the suspicion and disdain of native Puerto Ricans were the American ways Neoricans had adopted, which were often seen as overly assertive and brash on the island and marked them as foreigners. Rene Labarca, who worked for the Puerto Rican government's Planning Department, describes these differences:

When Puerto Ricans arrive in New York, they are immediately confronted with a very different world, a very hurried, harried, aggressive world. It has a great effect on them. They must conform and conform quickly if they are to survive.

When they come back, they are different. You can see it particularly in the women. In New York, these women have to become very aggressive—often to the point of threatening to use their fists—to get what they need for their children and themselves.[57]

As return migrants struggled to overcome cultural differences, their children—especially those who had spent their entire lives on the mainland—underwent their own difficult period of assimilation. The most debilitating factor for these young migrants was the language. They often spoke no Spanish, or if they did it was with a heavy accent. This problem worsened when students entered Puerto Rican classrooms. There, the children of return migrants faced the same kind of language barriers that their parents had faced as young students in American schools. Germán Díaz, a return migrant and parent, recalls her frustration:

> We who migrated to the United States in the 1940s and 1950s were shoved into the public system and told to sink or swim. . . . I return to Puerto Rico thirty years later and my son begins to relive the experiences. We are part of the reverse migration and now we find reverse discrimination.[58]

Divided by Jobs, United by Air

Reverse discrimination, cultural differences, and the language barrier were only

Born in the United States, the children of migrants returning to the island often faced language barriers in Puerto Rican classrooms like this one.

one set of problems return migrants had to deal with. By the early 1980s the island's recession-damaged economy was even shakier. Puerto Rico's unemployment rate spiraled out of control, in some regions growing as high as 50 percent. Good jobs were becoming increasingly scarce. Once again, the return migrants found themselves in a difficult situation. Although they had returned to their beloved homeland, making a living was next to impossible. Many families debated whether it was better to wait out the recession on the island, or pick up stakes and go back to the mainland, where the economy was slowly improving.

This was the dilemma facing Manny Ortíz and his family when the *New York Times* profiled them in 1984. Ortíz had first migrated to the Bronx with his parents when he was a small child. There, he went to school, met and married his wife, and had three daughters. In the early 1970s his parents returned to rural Puerto Rico. Ortíz and his family joined them there in 1977. Shortly after arriving on the island, Ortíz had been enthusiastic about the move and returning to his heritage. However, as Puerto Rico's economy slumped, Ortíz was laid off from his job as an electrician. Although he could have found other jobs, such as an electrician's assistant or a maintenance worker in a factory, he declined. These were low-paying jobs compared to what he was used to.

To solve this problem, Ortíz created a compromise. He wanted to return to New York where he could get a good-paying job, but he didn't want to uproot his daughters, who were still in school. So in 1982 Ortíz moved back to the mainland while his wife

and daughters remained in Puerto Rico. He rented an apartment and quickly secured a job as an electrician earning $900 a month, which was a small fortune compared to the $200 a week he would have been able to earn if he had found a job on the island. He sent most of his paycheck back to Puerto Rico.

Although this situation put a strain on the Ortíz family, it was not an uncommon arrangement among return migrants. They often had extended families living on both the mainland and the island, and they were able to shuttle between the two locations depending on which offered the best opportunities for work. When a family was divided between the island and the mainland, they looked to travel agencies to help their families stay in touch. Ortíz and thousands of workers in similar circumstances flew back to Puerto Rico every few months for short visits with their families. Travel agencies with signs advertising *pasajes* (passages) were common in Puerto Rican neighborhoods. The travel agencies specialized in arranging low-cost tickets for flights to the island. Airfare was such an important issue in New York's Puerto Rican community that when rates increased, politicians often became involved.

Caught in Cultural Limbo

The trend of return migration continued throughout the 1980s, especially among people in their twenties and thirties. As jobs became better on the mainland, migrants returned to the United States, and when the situation in Puerto Rico improved, they moved back to the island. However, the multiple moves between two different cultures began to take a toll on the migrants and contributed to what some Puerto Rican community leaders termed "cultural limbo."[59]

Cultural limbo manifested itself in different ways. The frequent moves prevented children from becoming established at a single school, for example. Making lasting and meaningful connections with friends and teachers was next to impossible. Language also posed difficulties. Often, young migrants could speak enough Spanish and English to get by, but did not have a mastery over either language.

Adults were also affected by the cultural limbo. Those who frequently moved back and forth with the goal of securing good jobs often had trouble finding work. This may have been in part because employers were reluctant to offer work to applicants who had an established pattern of moving every few months when a new opportunity arose. Hard-pressed to find work on the mainland, disappointed migrants returned to the island, and the cycle repeated itself.

Puerto Ricans living in the United States made frequent trips home to visit family.

A Long-Awaited Return

By the 1990s a new trend of return migrants began to emerge. No longer were they only twenty- and thirty-year-olds looking for work. Instead, these return migrants were senior citizens who had traveled to the United States as teenagers and young adults during the Great Migration. Although they had married, raised their children, and worked for decades in the United States, their hearts still belonged to the island of their birth. Indeed, for many migrants, returning felt like fulfilling an obligation to their homeland. Gilberto Gerena Valentín, who spent forty-nine years living in the United States, chose to return at the age of sixty-seven. "It's a duty, a historic duty to move back to where you came from,"[60] he says.

For others, the return trip was much more sentimental. They missed the sights, sounds, and smells of their childhood. María Rivera,

In the 1990s, many migrants returned to Puerto Rico as senior citizens. Some returned because they dearly missed such native traditions as a friendly outdoor game of dominoes.

who chose to return to the island at the age of sixty-one, wanted to return to simple pleasures in life such as being able to use fresh rather than frozen banana leaves to make a traditional Puerto Rican Christmas dish. And although she had to leave behind a sister and three grown children in the United States, she returned to siblings, aunts, uncles, and cousins. "When you leave your family and the country that you love," says Rivera, "you feel so happy going back."[61]

Like Rivera, Bartolo Figueroa left behind grown children to live out his dream of re-turning to his hometown of Patillas. Figueroa, like hundreds of other Puerto Rican migrants, had moved to the United States to take a job at the Bethlehem Steel Corporation in Pennsylvania. After working there for thirty years, he retired. At that point, returning to Patillas was on the top of his priority list. "I was not going to leave Patillas forever," says Figueroa. "Many people from my town and others nearby made that same promise, to return, but not all did. It's not easy leaving your children and not seeing your grandchildren. But this was what I was going to do from the beginning."[62]

CHAPTER FIVE

A Juggling Act

As America's Puerto Rican population ebbed and flowed over the twentieth century, a new situation began to arise. Unlike other immigrant populations that had little direct contact with their homeland and had taken on a more American identity, Puerto Ricans were actively balancing two cultures, two languages, and two homelands. Migrant Esmeralda Santiago describes this way of life:

I am a person who lives in two worlds. I am bilingual. I am bicultural. Sometimes I feel like a child jumping double dutch—two ropes [Puerto Rican and American identity] going in op-

posite directions very quickly. . . . It is a constant juggling, a constant jumping up and down, trying to be in one place or another, trying to understand am I responding here with the American part of me, or am I responding here with the Puerto Rican part of me. [63]

The juggling Santiago refers to is not a new phenomenon. It began when the first Puerto Rican migrants arrived more than one hundred years ago and is still going on today. Over the course of that time span, Puerto Rican communities across the United States have developed ways to preserve their

A JUGGLING ACT **67**

island heritage while still assimilating into their new homeland. By successfully performing this mental juggling act, the migrants have created a community with a blended identity; by weaving the Puerto Rican strands of their lives with the American ones, they have produced a tapestry that defines them as a distinct group within the nation.

From the construction of island-style *casitas* in the South Bronx to the colorful

A Puerto Rican family enjoys the 1993 Puerto Rican Day parade in Wilmington, Delaware.

Puerto Rican Day parades held in cities across the nation, the Puerto Rican identity is a complex blend of two very different worlds. However, the *casitas* and the parades are more than an outlet for the island spirit on the mainland. They are visible expressions that reinforce a bicultural identity, keeping it alive even among those second- and third-generation Puerto Rican Americans who have never visited the island and do not speak Spanish.

The Stain of the Plantain

Before adopting a bicultural identity, Puerto Ricans had to examine exactly what it meant to be an American, what it meant to be a Puerto Rican, and then, finally, what it meant to be a Puerto Rican American. This was not a simple task. Language, skin color, age, class, and birthplace all must join together to create the complex web of identity, and oftentimes these factors are at odds with each other.

Sonia Nieto has faced this struggle her entire life. Nieto was born and raised in the United States, although her parents were from Puerto Rico. Despite her fluent English and her American education, she always identified herself more as a Puerto Rican than an American. "When I am asked the inevitable question, 'What are you?'" says Nieto, "I always answer 'Puerto Rican.'"[64] However, Nieto's mainland upbringing had marked her as an American in ways she was unaware of:

Several years ago, I was jarred when speaking with an island-born Puerto Rican who commented that he could tell at first glance that I was born and raised in the United States simply by looking at my body language! Here I was, convinced that I was as Puerto Rican as any Puerto Rican, that I had *la mancha del plátano* (the stain of the plantain) firmly imprinted on my face and body, and yet he saw my American roots through it all. [65]

The issue of not only Puerto Rican identity, but also Latino identity in general, grew even more pronounced in 1999. That summer, the mainstream press began exploring Latinos, who had become America's fastest-growing ethnic group. On the radio, it was impossible to escape the music of Puerto Rican–born singer Ricky Martin as he belted out his number-one single "Livin' la Vida Loca" ("Livin' the Crazy Life"). At newsstands, cover stories such as "Pop Music Goes Latin" in *Time* magazine and "Latin U.S.A." in *Newsweek* appeared with pie charts, color-coded maps, line graphs, and interviews to educate Americans on the identity of this growing ethnic group.

Americans were fascinated by the bicultural lives Puerto Ricans and other Latinos were living. Some Americans began taking Spanish classes, and traditional Latino food became trendy. Companies began advertising to the Latino community and politicians began courting their votes. However, some in the community urged caution with pop culture's approach to the complex blending of Latino identities. "Don't try to understand Latinos through [Ricky Martin]," said Manuel Margaña, a college student. "It's like trying to figure out Americans by listening to the Backstreet Boys." [66]

Puerto Rican pop star Ricky Martin became a sensation in the United States in the late 1990s.

Fighting the Shark Stereotype

Ricky Martin was hardly the first stereotype Puerto Ricans had encountered in their quest to craft a bicultural identity. Perhaps one of the most enduring stereotypes was common more than forty years before Martin burst onto the pop culture scene in the United States. In September 1957 a musical play called *West Side Story* opened triumphantly

The Puerto Rican Barbie

In early 1997 Mattel began selling a Puerto Rican Barbie doll as part of its Dolls of the World line. The Puerto Rican Barbie, which has coffee-colored skin and straight hair, comes dressed in a traditional peasant outfit worn during colonial times.

The Puerto Rican Barbie, like the others in the Dolls of the World line, was meant to teach children about other cultures. Instead, it started a firestorm of controversy surrounding identity among Puerto Ricans living in the United States. Many criticized its European features and straight hair, and some said the outfit perpetuated a stereotype of a nineteenth-century Puerto Rican woman.

"Puerto Ricans are constantly probing their unresolved identity," said Puerto Rican sociology professor Victor Rodríguez in a 1997 interview with the *Times Union* of Albany, New York. "Most of our great literature essentially asks, 'Who am I?' So to introduce a doll, a doll that looks like it has no trace of African ancestry, to a group of young Puerto Rican females who are at a crucial age in the formation of their identity, this becomes a very serious issue."

However, not everyone was quite so quick to judge the new doll negatively. Amanda, an eight-year-old who lives just outside of San Juan, has nothing but praise for the Puerto Rican Barbie she received as a Christmas gift. "I like it more because she's from my country," says Amanda. "It's my favorite."

on Broadway. The award-winning play, featuring Leonard Bernstein's music and Stephen Sondheim's lyrics—and the movie version that followed—forever altered the perception of Puerto Rican identity in the United States.

The story is a modern version of William Shakespeare's *Romeo and Juliet* that pits a Puerto Rican gang, the Sharks, against an American gang, the Jets. As the two gangs prepare for a rumble, a Puerto Rican girl named María falls in love with a member of the Jets, Tony. Throughout the musical, Puerto Rican culture in the 1950s is vividly, if misleadingly, portrayed as characters dance, fight, and sing songs about their experiences as newcomers to the country. However, aspects of the Puerto Rican lifestyle were represented in *West Side Story* in ways that many considered to paint Puerto Rican men as gangsters and women as either vixens or victims. As the movie made its way across the United States, these stereotypes were perpetuated. And as Puerto Ricans struggled to claim their bicultural identity, the movie continued to get in the way.

"The girls [in my class] had seen Carmen Miranda movies and had heard *West Side Story,* and that's what they thought life was like for Puerto Ricans—the song and dance gang wars," recalls migrant Luisita López Torregrosa. "So I became the Carmen Miranda of the sophomore class, Chita Rivera in *West Side Story,* fitting the picture they had of me."[67] After moving to the mainland, critic Alberto Sandoval also found the stereotypes from the movie hard to flee. "And how can I forget those who upon my arrival would start tapping flamenco steps and squealing: 'I like to be in America'? [one of Sondheim's lyrics]," says Sandoval. "As the years passed by I grew accustomed to their actions and reactions to my presence. I would smile and ignore the stereotype of Puerto Ricans that Hollywood promotes."[68]

Today, the influence of *West Side Story* on the complex identity of Puerto Ricans is still present. Indeed, author Frances Negrón-Muntaner goes so far as to say,

There are cultural icons that never seem to die no matter how much dirt you throw on them. And the multifaced *West Side Story*—Broadway show, Hollywood film, staple of high school drama programs, inspiration for the 2000 Gap campaign featuring "the latest spring styles and colors of the Khakis and the Jeans," and possible remake featuring "real" Puerto Rican cast—refuses to bow out after way too many curtain calls.[69]

The Puerto Rican Day Parade

If watching *West Side Story* and listening to Ricky Martin cannot provide an authentic insight into the bicultural identity of a Puerto Rican, attending a Puerto Rican Day parade can at least edge closer to

With an estimated three million spectators, New York City's annual Puerto Rican Day parade has become the nation's largest ethnic parade.

it. The parade is one of the oldest and most visible forms of Puerto Rican biculturalism. It began in New York City in 1958, when approximately two hundred thousand people gathered to watch it. In recent years, as Puerto Rican flags wave in the wind, island folk music reverberates through the streets, and beauty queens wave to the crowds, an estimated 3 million people enjoy the event.

The parade has always been about more than entertainment, however. In an effort to reinforce ties between migrants and the island, every year Puerto Rican mayors and other politicians would journey to New York City to take part in the parade. "The Puerto Rican Parade," says Puerto Rico's longtime governor Luis Muñoz Marín, "is a manifestation of the advancement and progress of Puerto Ricans in New York and the spirit of improvement of our culture and our people."[70] Indeed, New York's Puerto Rican Day parade proved to be a powerful outlet for the community's pride and identity. Before long, other American cities with large Puerto Rican populations continued this tradition. From Philadelphia to Chicago, Puerto Rican leaders joined together to create their own Puerto Rican Day parades.

Today, these parades continue to draw masses of spectators. In New York City the event has become so large that it is credited as the nation's largest ethnic parade. Whether they are recent migrants or have lived in America their entire lives, whether they are native Spanish speakers or native English speakers, the parades provide an outlet for people to declare their Puerto Rican heritage in all its different forms. After riding in the Puerto Rican Day parade,

singer Ednita Nazario commented on this phenomenon:

What I felt when I was on that float, what I saw—the pride, the sheer joy that I experienced by seeing those millions of people who sometimes didn't even speak the language, didn't speak Spanish, but who had that strong sense of pride, gave me the most incredible sense of joy because they weren't born in Puerto Rico, but Puerto Rico was born in them.[71]

Other Outpourings

Perhaps the Puerto Rican Day parade is the jewel in the crown of the bicultural identity, but other events such as festivals and museum exhibits are also vitally important.

One of the best known of these festivals is the Feast of Saint John the Baptist, the patron saint of San Juan. By the 1960s it had become the leading event among New York's large community of Catholic Puerto Ricans. They celebrated by attending Mass, as well as partaking in other events such as choir performances and dances. "Saint John unites us and protects us," says migrant Amalia Betanzos. "Thus although we're separated by great distances, we form a single people. . . . This is a continuity with [the island], although the sea separates us. . . . Here, in New York, Puerto Rico lives, hopes, creates, prays, and manifests itself."[72] The Feast of Saint John the Baptist was soon joined by other events.

Today, dozens of festivals around the nation celebrate the Puerto Rican community with music, food, and art, but these are not

Puerto Rican American schoolchildren wear crowns to celebrate the annual Three Kings Day parade in New York City, another of the city's distinctly Puerto Rican festivals.

the only outlets through which Puerto Ricans express their bicultural pride. In 1969, for example, leaders in the artistic community founded El Museo del Barrio. It is New York's only museum dedicated solely to artwork with Puerto Rican, Caribbean, and Latin American roots. It provides a forum for visitors to view visual artwork related to their heritage.

Other visual elements of Puerto Rican identity, such as the *jíbaro,* are also present across the United States. The *jíbaro* is a poor, uneducated farmer. However, he is also proud, self-sufficient, and skilled at working the land and caring for animals. The *jíbaro,* along with the straw hat he wears, has come to represent Puerto Ricanness on the main-

land. The *jíbaro*'s image has appeared everywhere from local schools, where students dress up to represent their heritage, to exhibits at the Smithsonian Institution.

Constructing *Casitas*

Another way the blending of Puerto Rican and American cultures has manifested itself is in the construction of *casitas* in New York. In Spanish, the word *casita* means "little house," and they were primarily small dwellings. On the island, poor families would build *casitas* on whatever land they could find, often near a riverbank. Since they did not own the land, the *casita* dwellers knew that at any time the government could ask them to move. For this reason, they made the *casitas* portable.

The *casita* culture came to New York in the 1970s. During that time, a Puerto Rican named Don José Manuel "Chema" Soto began to clear one of the vacant lots that were plentiful in the South Bronx during this time. After the work was done, he and some friends had a bonfire in the lot and began to see its full potential. Before long, they were constructing a small but cheery island-style *casita* and traditional garden on a desolate, abandoned lot in America's largest city.

Soto's *casita* and garden, now known as the Rincón Criollo Community Center, drew an unexpected amount of attention from neighbors. It gradually began hosting community events, including cookouts and concerts featuring traditional Puerto Rican music. Throughout the 1980s *casitas* began popping up in other areas of the South Bronx as well as East Harlem. Like Soto had done before, leaders cleared garbage, abandoned cars, and other debris from the lots and replaced them with *casitas* and gardens for use by the community.

The *casitas* have become beloved landmarks of the Puerto Rican community. They provide a safe place for children to play, for elders to start a game of dominoes, or for families to listen to Puerto Rican folk music. *Casitas* succeeded in blending rural island traditions with the fast-paced life of

Speaking Spanglish

In 2003 Ilan Stavans, a professor of Latin American and Latino Culture at Amherst College in Massachusetts, compiled a list of Spanglish terms in a book titled *Spanglish: The Making of a New American Language*. These terms are neither completely English nor completely Spanish. Instead, they are a fusion of the two languages and allow Puerto Ricans, as well as other people who know both Spanish and English, a great deal of flexibility in their everyday communications. Samples of Spanglish words identified by Stavans are listed below.

bagaje (bah-GA-cheh): baggage
beismen (BEIS-men): basement

caleraidi (ka-ler-AY-dee): caller ID
castumar (cas-TOO-mar): customer
deiof (dey-OF): day off
esnack (es-NAK): snack food
foni (FO-nee): funny
gom (GOM): bubblegum
hangear (han-GEHAR): to hang out
kartón (kar-TON): cardboard
laca (LA-kah): door lock
lonch (LONCH): midday meal
nai (NAY): nice
nerdio (ner-DIOH): nerd
polís (po-LEES): police
poquebú (po-ke-BOO): pocketbook
queki (keh-KEE): cake
ruki (ROOH-kee): novice
súper (SOO-per): supermarket
yarda (YAR-da): backyard

New York City. "Just looking at this place [Rincón Criollo], I went through a transition," says migrant Louis Ramos. "Like a rebirth. It tapped my memory and brought back my parents in Puerto Rico. I never felt like I belonged in New York City—there weren't any palm trees, the people didn't speak my language. But when I came here, I didn't feel out of place."[73]

Spanglish

The *casitas,* a complex blend of new and old traditions, are not the only way Puerto Ricans are able to bridge the gap between their two cultures. Language is another area where the influences of island and mainland tug migrants in different directions. For many, language is not only a way to communicate, but it is also a badge of identity that reveals itself as soon as a person speaks. For Puerto Ricans, this badge can take many forms. Of course, Spanish is the first language of many migrants and English is what they quickly learn when they arrive on American soil. But there is also a third language option, known as Spanglish.

As its name implies, Spanglish is a blend of Spanish and English words, grammar, and sentence structure. Puerto Ricans and other Spanish-speaking immigrants use it as a way to combine parts of each language in a new way, depending whom they are with, what is most convenient, and what language best represents what they'd like to say. *"Me likea el rufo"* (My roof is leaking), *"downlodear"* (to download on a computer), and *"Loisiada"* (New York's Lower East Side) are just a few examples of how this hybrid language has manifested itself among migrants.[74]

Spanglish is also used as a tool to cope with the difficulties of flip-flopping between two worlds. "You work all day speaking English," says a bilingual Puerto Rican migrant, "and then you go home and speak Spanish for only a few hours in the evening. Or if you watch the TV it is even worse. So you begin to forget your Spanish words because you don't practice them enough. And if you can't think of a Spanish word you use the English word instead, and pretty soon you have a lot of English words in your vocabulary."[75]

However, there are many purists who see Spanglish as a handicap for Puerto Ricans and other Spanish-speaking immigrants. They argue that if migrants rely on Spanglish to get by, they may never develop a mastery of either English or Spanish. They argue that lacking fluency in either language is a trap, putting Spanglish speakers at a distinct disadvantage. As a result, many parents and teachers correct children so they speak proper Spanish or proper English, not Spanglish.

Spanglish, however, is a form of identity. "Spanglish is proof that Latinos have a culture that is made up of two parts. It's not that you are Latino or American," says Ilan Stavans, a professor who has studied Spanglish and its role in migrant communication. "You live on the hyphen, in between. That's what Spanglish is all about, a middle ground."[76]

And Your Grandmother, Where Is She?

Speaking Spanglish is one way Puerto Ricans have managed to balance two cultures.

In Puerto Rico, where most inhabitants, like these young girls, are of mixed heritage, racial discrimination is less common than in the United States.

However, some aspects of the balancing act are more difficult to grapple with, especially when it comes to race. On the island, where descendants of native Taíno Indians, Spanish conquistadors, and African slaves have intermarried over the centuries, almost everyone is of mixed heritage. Although Puerto Ricans are certainly aware of skin color, it is seldom a source of prejudice or discrimination, and race, in general, is not a major issue.

On the mainland, where racial distinctions receive more attention, Puerto Ricans may not fit into the neatly defined categories of "white" and "nonwhite" historically used in the United States. Instead, they may rely on an island system of classifying race, which is much more flexible. Puerto Ricans

use a combination of categories—hair texture, facial features, and a spectrum of skin color from white to brown to black—to create a racial identity. The result, however, does not always translate easily into American society.

When Marta Cruz-Janzen arrived in the United States from Ponce, Puerto Rico, she found that she was being judged on her dark skin color more than ever before. "I remember I started getting advice from people. Some said, 'Emphasize the fact that you are Latina,'" Cruz-Janzen says. But she didn't always feel Latina. Sometimes she identified more with her African roots. "But then I would go to the African American groups and they would say I was not black enough."[77] In the end, Cruz-Janzen coined her own term to describe herself and her mixed Latino and African roots: *Latinegra.* It is a blend of the words *Latina* (meaning a woman from Latin America) and *negro* (which means "black" in Spanish.)

Cruz-Janzen is not the only Puerto Rican who redefined her racial identity upon arriving in the United States. The 2000 Census revealed a shift in racial categories among Puerto Ricans. On the island, 81 percent of Puerto Ricans classified themselves as white. The respondents living on the mainland had a much different take on the situation, where only 46 percent identified themselves as white and 47 percent said they were "some other race." According to Jorge Duany, a professor at the University of Puerto Rico, this shift happens because on the mainland Puerto Ricans "rarely used conventional U.S. terms to describe their racial identity and preferred to say that they were Spanish, Puerto Rican, Boricua, or trigueño [literally, the color of wheat]." [78]

Beyond Black and White

The issue of race among Puerto Ricans is a complex one. Puerto Ricans use nearly twenty different terms to describe skin color. Jorge Duany, a professor of anthropology at the University of Puerto Rico, has assembled these terms into a list in his book *The Puerto Rican Nation on the Move.* The list demonstrates the broad spectrum of skin color among Puerto Ricans and how this translates into a broad range of identities beyond black and white.

Blanco(a): White

Blanquito(a): Literally, little white; figuratively, elitist, upper class

Colorado(a): Redheaded, reddish skin

Rubio(a): Blond

Cano(a): Blond, fair-skinned

Jincho(a): Pale skinned; sometimes used pejoratively

Blanco(a) con raja: Literally, white with a crack; white with some visible black features

Jabao(a): Fair skinned with curly hair

Trigueño(a): Literally, wheat-colored or brunette; usually light mulatto

Moreno(a): Dark-skinned; usually dark mulatto

Mulato(a): Mixed race; rarely used in public

Indio(a): Literally, Indian; brown-skinned with straight hair

Café con leche: Literally, coffee with milk; tan or brown-skinned

Piel canela: Literally, cinnamon skin; tan or brown-skinned

Prieto(a): Dark-skinned; usually derogatory

Grifo(a): Dark-skinned with kinky hair; usually derogatory

De color: Euphemism for black; usually meaning black

Negro(a): Black; rarely used as a direct term of reference

Negrito(a): Literally, little black; often used as a term of endearment

In fact, when it comes to race many Puerto Ricans frown upon their fellow islanders who try to identify themselves as too white, too Americanized. When this happens, Puerto Ricans may pointedly ask, *¿Y tú abuela, dónde está?* (And your grandmother, where is she?). The question is a reminder that Puerto Ricans identifying as white most likely have an African or Taíno relative somewhere in their family tree. The question is meant to prevent people from forgetting their rich ethnic heritage.

From Taíno Clubs to Turkeys

For many, asking *¿Y tú abuela, dónde está?* may be just one part of the Puerto Rican identity equation. For many, the process of discovering and living out this bicultural identity in the midst of mainstream America is a lifelong quest. It is a process that is riddled with twists and turns, leaving many Puerto Ricans to vacillate between two worlds before realizing they can successfully live in both.

In their journey to reclaim parts of their Latino identity, some Puerto Ricans are seeking ways to blend their Taíno heritage with life in modern America. One such person is Neryda González, an American executive of Puerto Rican descent. She has worked to reconcile her ancient indigenous heritage with the fast-paced American lifestyle. For example, she may wear a modern business suit with traditional Taíno elements such as a red coral necklace. She is also active in a Taíno club, the Village of the Gourd, where she goes by the name Guatunaru, which means "fire woman."

Puerto Ricans whose Taíno heritage is slight or uncertain may seek to incorporate their Puerto Rican roots through another channel: food. Many families combine mainstream American foods with traditional island flavors. On Thanksgiving Day, for example, a Puerto Rican family might serve a traditional American turkey dinner. However, the turkey might have a stuffing made from plantains, a staple in the Puerto Rican diet, rather than the American version made from stale bread. It is a typical blending of island and mainland tastes.

A Proud, Complex People

This bicultural identity is reinforced by the relationship between the United States and Puerto Rico. "It's an incredibly complex community," says Félix Matos Rodríguez, the director of the Center for Puerto Rican Studies at New York City's Hunter College. Matos Rodríguez elaborates on this idea:

> You have third-generation Puerto Ricans in the United States whose connection to the island is minimal, but who are very much Puerto Rican in the way they understand themselves and conduct their daily lives. You have Puerto Ricans on the island who have never migrated, and are never going to migrate. You have to make room for the complexity of all of these different experiences within the umbrella of Puerto Ricanness.[79]

This complexity was compounded when the status debate, which Governor Muñoz

Puerto Rico's commonwealth status allows the island to assemble Olympic teams like the successful 2004 men's basketball team.

Marín had declared to be over in 1967, resurfaced. After Puerto Ricans elected Pedro Rosselló as governor in 1992, the status debate heated up again. Rosselló wanted to see the island become America's fifty-first state. To achieve this, he arranged for two plebiscites, one in 1993 and another one in 1998. Both times, Puerto Ricans voted to keep the island a commonwealth.

The plebiscites had been more than a vote on government, however. They had also been a vote on identity. True, if Puerto Ricans were to give up their status as a commonwealth and become a state they would gain benefits, such as being able to vote for the president. However, many Puerto Ricans believed the benefits did not outweigh the risks. For example, many

Puerto Ricans feared their island would lose its native language and culture if it became a state. They would also no longer be able to assemble their own Olympic teams or enter their own contestants in the Miss Universe pageant, both sources of pride on the island as well as the mainland.

Aníbal Acevedo Vilá, a pro-commonwealth political leader, summed up this complex reality that spans the island and the mainland. He addressed a crowd of Puerto Ricans who had assembled after the 1998 plebiscite and told them, "Here is a people proud of its history. Here is a people proud of its relationship with the United States. Here is a people proud of its citizenship, and also proud of its Puerto Ricanness."[80]

CHAPTER SIX

An American Success Story

fter decades of carving out a bicultural identity and working to emerge from under the shadow of the "Puerto Rican problem," the Puerto Rican community has become powerful and established. Its neighborhoods, once considered dangerous and unsavory, have been revitalized. And its influence has grown to reach mainstream culture. Today, Puerto Rican headliners such as Jennifer Lopez, Geraldo Rivera, and Gigi Fernández have become household names across the nation. Other Puerto Ricans have become successful in high-profile positions in the government, the military, and the world of business. Theirs is truly an American success story.

Overcoming the Ghetto Star Reputation

Success was not achieved overnight; it took years of hard work for Puerto Ricans to break into traditional mainstream holdouts such as the English-language media. During the early years of the migration, Spanish-language radio programs and newspapers were the only media outlets that would hire Puerto Ricans. Despite the limitations, Puerto Ricans were successful in these fields. In 1924, for example, Puerto Rican–born migrant Julio Roqué started a popular radio program called *Revista Roqué.* It featured music from the island that was performed live by local musicians.

Revista Roqué was followed by numerous other variety and talk shows in the 1940s and 1950s, and they garnered huge Puerto Rican audiences.

Despite the increased accessibility of the airwaves, however, the Puerto Rican community was barely represented in mainstream, English-language media outlets. The coverage they did receive was often quite negative. Marifé Hernández, a Puerto Rican pioneer in the field of television during the 1970s, comments:

Rita Moreno

In Humacao, a small town on the edge of Puerto Rico's El Yunque rain forest, a girl named Rosa "Rosita" Alverio was born in 1932. She came from a family of *jíbaros* and spent her earliest years living on a farm. Then, plagued by the hardships of the Great Depression, five-year-old Rosita and her mother left Humacao for New York.

The young *jíbara* easily fit into life in New York and her talent was soon recognized. At age seven, Rosita made her first public performance as a dancer in a New York club. At eleven, Rosita was working in the film industry by dubbing English-language movies into Spanish. Just two years later, she landed her first role on Broadway.

Now known as Rita Moreno, the girl from Humacao was on a path to greatness. During her work as an actress, she has become the only woman ever to win an Oscar (*West Side Story,* 1962), a Grammy (*The Electric Company* soundtrack, 1972), a Tony (*The Ritz,* 1975), and an Emmy (*Sesame Street,* 1977, and *The Rockford Files,* 1978).

Despite her fame, Moreno remained true to her roots. In remarks that appear in *Adiós, Borinquen Querida,* Moreno says,

"I am Latin and know what it is to feel ignored and alone because you are different. When you are ignored you have lost your sense of identity. So I can be the only Latin on this show and my presence there can tell a lot of children and some adults, 'Yes, we do exist, we have value.'"

Puerto Rican actress Rita Moreno won an Oscar in 1962 for her performance in West Side Story.

By the early 1960s, every major magazine, newspaper, and television station in the New York metropolitan area had done a series or at least a feature story on the Puerto Ricans. Whether you read about the gang wars between Puerto Rican youths, saw the pictures of those thin, dark haired Puerto Rican girls dressed in skimpy summer dresses in twenty degree winter weather in magazines, or witnessed the rats and dirt in a Puerto Rican home courtesy of a TV screen—Puerto Ricans had become the ghetto stars of the New York media.[81]

By the 1970s, however, a new force was on the horizon that would put a Puerto Rican face on the media. The name of this force was Geraldo Rivera. Rivera was the child of a Puerto Rican father and a Jewish mother. He grew up in New York City, and watching

Shown here with his wife, Geraldo Rivera is best known for his work as a broadcast journalist and as host of his own syndicated talk show.

the difficulties his father faced as a migrant, he vowed to rise above them himself. In 1969 Rivera graduated from law school and began taking on Puerto Rican clients such as the Young Lords. When he learned that the American Broadcasting Company (ABC) was looking for a bilingual reporter, he applied for the job. After a few months of training, Rivera began working as a journalist and gained national exposure. He reported for WABC-TV's *Eyewitness News* in New York City, *Good Morning America,* and *20/20.* He has also hosted a nationally syndicated talk show, *The Geraldo Rivera Show,* and a news program called *At Large with Geraldo Rivera* on Fox News.

While Rivera brought a high-profile Puerto Rican presence to English-language newscasts, other parts of the media were also following suit. Gradually, more and more Puerto Ricans were starring in mainstream television programs and movies. Sonia Manzano, for example, is a Bronx-born actress of Puerto Rican descent who has played the character of María on the children's program *Sesame Street* for more than three decades. She's not alone. Standout Puerto Rican actors such as Rita Moreno, the late Raúl Julia, Erik Estrada, Rosie Pérez, Jimmy Smits, Héctor Elizondo, Jennifer Lopez, Benicio del Toro, and the late José Ferrer rose to fame through mainstream movies, plays, or television shows.

As these actors rose to stardom in English-language roles, Puerto Ricans continued to maintain their presence in America's Spanish-language media as well. Rossana Rosado, for example, is the publisher of *El Diario/La Prensa,* the nation's oldest Spanish-language newspaper, which also happens to have the largest readership of any Spanish-language daily newspaper in the northeastern United States. The Bronx-born Rosado understands the important role the newspaper plays not only in keeping New York's Latino community aware of current events, but also in preserving its Spanish heritage. "As a newspaper, *El Diario/La Prensa* does not only have the duty to inform our readers," says Rosado, "but we have the social responsibility to educate them and other New Yorkers about our history."[82]

Serving the United States

In the world of mainstream media, Puerto Ricans built upon the successes of past generations to gain a place of prominence. So, too, did this happen in the world of public service, from participating in the U.S. military to passing federal laws. However, this was not an easy task. Nearly all who wanted to serve the United States in any capacity, from soldiers to politicians, met with obstacles.

For example, all Puerto Ricans are eligible for service in the U.S. military because they are citizens. Thousands of Puerto Rican soldiers served honorably in World Wars I and II. Their outfit was officially known as the 65th U.S. Infantry. However, military leaders frequently dismissed it as the Rum and Coke Brigade and considered its soldiers to be inferior to those from the mainland.

That mentality changed when the 65th U.S. Infantry served in the Korean War. During that conflict, its soldiers earned a reputation for being courageous and reliable. Since then, soldiers of Puerto Rican descent have bravely served in all of America's military conflicts. They have also risen to positions of power within the military. Horacio Rivero, for example, became not only the first Puerto Rican but also the first Latino to be promoted to the rank of four-star admiral in the U.S. Navy.

Just as Puerto Ricans overcame obstacles before becoming successful in the military, they also faced obstacles when entering the political arena. Early on, Puerto Ricans had some success in entering mainstream politics. Oscár García Rivera was elected to the New York State legislature in 1937, for example. For the most part, however, Puerto Rican leaders and politicians had focused on improving their communities through civic groups, such as hometown clubs, rather than through state and federal positions. With a few exceptions, the Puerto Rican community remained largely ignored by powerful mainstream politicians.

However, that changed in 1970 when a Puerto Rican politician made history. That year, voters from New York elected Herman Badillo to Congress. Winning that election made Badillo the first Puerto Rican to serve as a U.S. representative. Other community leaders soon built upon his success. They founded organizations such as the National Puerto Rican Coalition, the National Congress for Puerto Rican Rights, and the Institute for Puerto Rican Policy to represent the community. And, like Badillo, other Puerto Ricans gained political power by winning important local and national elections. Elected officials such as Robert García, Nydia Velázquez, José Serrano, and Luis Gutiérrez have brought the Puerto

Rican perspective to the national government.

Raise Your Flag!

Just as politicians and soldiers have overcome barriers to succeed in the United States, so, too, have Puerto Rican athletes. Athletics are not taken lightly among Puerto Ricans on the island or the mainland. Seeing Puerto Rican athletes succeed is an immense source of pride and spirit that is summed up in the lyrics to Puerto Rico's official Olympic anthem:

> *Por ti, por mi* / For you, for me,
> *sin razas, sin fronteras,* / without races, without borders,
> *Puerto Rico* / Puerto Rico
> *!Levanta tu bandera!* / Raise your flag![83]

Puerto Rican athletics have a long history in the United States. Some of the island's first athletes to arrive on the mainland were baseball players. Baseball was introduced to Puerto Rico in the late nineteenth century, and before long a great enthusiasm for the sport spread across the island. Puerto Rico exported its first major league player, Hiram Bithorn, in 1942. The next year, Bithorn was followed in the major leagues by fellow Puerto Rican Luis Rodríguez Olmo.

While Bithorn and Rodríguez Olmo were able to play in the majors, many Puerto Ricans were not. Puerto Rican players with dark skin were allowed to play only in America's Negro Leagues during the years when professional baseball teams were segregated. When the major leagues

Roberto Clemente

On August 18, 1934, one of Puerto Rico's baseball legends was born just outside of San Juan. That legend was Roberto Clemente. Clemente was a fantastic all-around athlete, but his passion was baseball. His skills were quickly recognized, and he played in amateur leagues on the island. Then, in 1955, Clemente was drafted by the Pittsburgh Pirates. During his years as a Pirate, Clemente had three thousand hits and a batting average of .317. He was named an all-star four times, was chosen as the most valuable player of 1966, and was inducted into the Baseball Hall of Fame in 1973.

Despite these successes, being a black Latino player in the predominantly white league presented tremendous challenges. Sportswriters, for example, would make fun of Clemente's thick accent in their columns. He was also faced with insulting questions, such as one person who asked him if he wore a loincloth while on the island.

These difficulties inspired Clemente to root out racism in baseball. In a March 31, 2002, *Orlando Sentinel* article, Clemente's comments from years earlier appear. "Latin-American Negro ballplayers are treated today much like all Negroes were treated in baseball in the early days of the broken color barrier," said Clemente. "They are subjected to prejudices and stamped with generalizations. Because they speak Spanish among themselves, they are set off as a minority within a minority, and they bear the brunt of the sport's remaining racial prejudices. 'They're all lazy, look for the easy way, the short cut' is one charge. 'They have no guts' is another." Clemente's crusade to end racism in baseball was cut short when he tragically died in a plane crash in December 1972.

Roberto Clemente was inducted into the Baseball Hall of Fame in 1973.

Roberto Alomar is one of the biggest names in baseball today.

took a job as a caddy at a golf course. There, he developed a passion for the game, using the branches of guava trees as clubs to hit tin cans that had been crushed into balls. Despite his humble beginnings, Rodríguez's talent couldn't be doubted. In 1960 he joined the Professional Golfers Association of America (PGA). Over the course of his career, Rodríguez won eight PGA tournaments and twenty-two PGA senior events.

In the world of tennis, a young woman named Beatriz "Gigi" Fernández made history in 1992 at the Olympic Games in Barcelona, Spain. In Barcelona Fernández played doubles for the U.S. tennis team and became the first Puerto Rican ever to win an Olympic gold medal. Though Fernández played for the U.S. team, her thoughts were not far from her beloved island. After her victory, Fernández announced, "I'm very proud for Puerto Rico. I'm very proud for the U.S. I'm very proud."[84]

Climbing the Corporate Ladder

For Puerto Ricans, leadership in the world of business, just as in athletics, lagged their migration to the mainland by decades. This was largely because many first-generation migrants, being unskilled workers, were relegated to low-level positions with little room for advancement. Characteristically, many of these migrants encouraged their children to do well in school and get a good education so they would be better off. Gradually, graduation rates from high schools, universities, and technical colleges increased among second- and third-generation Puerto

were desegregated in 1947, they were able to sign some of the island's most prominent players, such as Roberto Clemente. Today, Puerto Rican players such as Roberto Alomar, Sandy Alomar Jr., Juan González, Bernie Williams, and Ivan Rodríguez have become standouts in major league baseball.

Puerto Ricans have also excelled in other sports as well. In the world of golf, for example, Juan "Chi Chi" Rodríguez has become renowned across the globe. Rodríguez grew up in a poor family and spent hours working in sugarcane fields. At age six, he

Ricans. With that advanced education came new success stories, this time in corporate America.

Puerto Ricans have held leadership positions in companies as diverse as Johnson & Johnson, the world's largest producer of health-care products, to Scientific Atlanta, a Fortune 500 company that provides high-tech products such as cable, broadband, and satellite communication systems. Other Puerto Ricans have succeeded by forming their own businesses. John "Jellybean" Benitez, for example, began his own record-producing business called Jellybean Productions, Inc. Through his company, Benitez has produced songs for international recording stars including Madonna, Michael Jackson, Whitney Houston, and Paul McCartney.

Other Puerto Rican business leaders have found success by expanding their island-based businesses to the mainland. One of those businesses is Banco Popular. It began offering banking services to islanders in 1893. By 1961 the bank had established its first branch in the United States. Today, it operates nearly one hundred branches on the mainland and is the largest Hispanic financial services franchise. "Throughout our 110-year history our mission has been

Pictured with his family in New York, John "Jellybean" Benitez is a successful record producer and owner of Jellybean Productions.

to make dreams happen for the Puerto Rican community,"[85] says the bank's president, Richard Carrión.

The Sounds of Puerto Rico

Unlike business or politics, the world of music was one in which Puerto Ricans gained acceptance almost immediately upon arriving in the United States. Hundreds of professionally trained musicians journeyed from Puerto Rico to the mainland during the early years of migration. This was especially true during the years of the Great Depression, when people on the island barely had enough money to buy food and paying to hear a professional musician was a luxury many could not afford.

Unable to find work on the island, Puerto Rican musicians moved to New York in the hope that conditions there might prove more favorable. Puerto Rico's most talented musicians, singers, conductors, and composers found work in the city's popular bands and orchestras. Influenced by the sounds they heard on the mainland, the musicians began experimenting. They blended traditional Caribbean and Latin American rhythms like the mambo, cha-cha, and rumba with American sounds like jazz, rock, and blues. By the 1950s Puerto Rican musicians in New York had succeeded in creating a new and tremendously popular style of music: salsa.

Salsa music has fast, danceable rhythms. It is played on a large variety of instruments that reflect the music's fusion of Puerto Rican and American styles. Instruments from American bands and orchestras, such as horns and bass, join island instruments such as claves (a pair of wooden sticks), maracas (rattles made from gourds), timbales (drums), and guiros (hollowed out gourds played with a scraper). Tito Puente, who gained fame in the 1950s, was the first well-known salsa musician. Since that time, salsa music's popularity has grown considerably and has brought this Puerto Rican music into the mainstream.

The newest face of salsa music, Marc Anthony, grew up in Spanish Harlem, and in 1998 became the first solo salsa singer to perform in Madison Square Garden. Since that time, his popularity—as well as the popularity of salsa—has reached new heights.

Shown here with Puerto Rican actress Rosie Pérez, Marc Anthony is a critically acclaimed salsa musician.

Anthony has released six albums in Spanish and two in English, with sales of more than 5.6 million copies. It's not just fans that love Anthony. The critics have also recognized this salsa musician's talent with two Latin Grammy Awards, one for his 1998 album *Contra la Corriente* and another for his 1999 hit song "I Need to Know."

While Anthony was belting out salsas, two other Puerto Rican musicians—Ricky Martin and Jennifer Lopez—were also rising to stardom with their Latin-influenced pop sounds. In 1999 Martin's first English single, "Livin' la Vida Loca," skyrocketed to the number-one slot on the Billboard charts. That same year, Lopez burst onto the music scene when she released her first album, *On the Six*. While the success of artists like Anthony, Martin, and Lopez has reached the mainstream, it still has its roots in Puerto Rican culture. "I remember being two years old and being put on the table and—in Spanish they say *menéalo*, but it means 'shake it, shake it,'" says Lopez. "I think I was probably dancing out of the womb. We are a very musical people, a very passionate people."[86]

Exodus from the City

While musicians, business leaders, and politicians were writing the next chapter in the Puerto Rican American success story, changes were happening within the community. One of the most noticeable of these changes centered on the heart of the Puerto Rican community: El Barrio. Once considered the cradle of the community, it had evolved into a difficult place to live. The cost of living there rose, while at the same time

Now famous as both a rock star and actress, Jennifer Lopez made her American debut with Latin-influenced pop songs in 1999.

the neighborhood took a downward turn. Aurora Flores, who grew up in El Barrio and still lives there today, comments on the area's decline by saying, "I remember when people used to get dressed to come to El Barrio, and then I remember when the elevators stopped working in our building and I had to step over junkies on the way to school."[87]

It wasn't just El Barrio that was facing a decline. Throughout New York City's Puerto Rican neighborhoods, people were packing up their belongings. "It's almost like New York City, as important as it is in the history of the Puerto Rican migration in the United States, became a dead end, economically, for many Puerto Ricans," [88] says Angelo Falcón, a leader in New York's Puerto Rican community. By the late 1990s Puerto Ricans were leaving the city in large numbers. It was, according to the 2000 Census, the first time in history that the Puerto Rican population in New York City had declined.

Their reasons for moving were varied, but most had grown weary of life in a large urban area. The expense, crime, crowding, and swift pace of life associated with the city had worn them down. They wanted more for their families, such as quality public schools and open areas where their children could play safely. Puerto Ricans were settling in suburbs and small towns across the nation, from Smiths, Alabama, to Lake in the Hills, Illinois.

However, the region with the fastest-growing Puerto Rican population between 1990 and 2000 was central Florida. During that time, ten thousand Puerto Ricans moved to Orlando alone. Other cities in central Florida also saw major growth. Kissimmee's Puerto Rican population increased by 174 percent and Brandon, a suburb of Tampa, saw a 339 percent increase. Given its warm climate and an affordable cost of living, it's not surprising that many Puerto Ricans were lured to the Sunshine State.

Ray Cruz was one such Puerto Rican attracted to Florida. In 1995 he moved his family from Queens, New York, to Tampa, Florida. "I spent all my life in New York and was never able to buy a home there," says Cruz, "I bought one here six months after we arrived." He continues, "We would never move back. It's not that we hate New York, but Florida is home for us. We're really happy here." [89]

Reclaiming El Barrio

As this exodus occurred, El Barrio—which had stood as a symbol of the Puerto Rican community in New York City for half a century—was becoming less Puerto Rican every day. Groups of newly arrived immigrants from West Africa, the Dominican Republic, and Mexico began to replace Puerto Ricans in the neighborhood. In 1999 author Craig Horowitz noted,

> Population shifts have begun to threaten several decades of Puerto Rican dominance in the neighborhood. The changes are immediately apparent on 116th Street, which is known in the neighborhood simply as the strip. . . . Though the street signs on the strip say Luis Muñoz Marín Boulevard—honoring the first governor of Puerto Rico—the store signs around Fifth Avenue all have West African names now. When you head east over to Third Avenue, you walk right into what is called Little Puebla, for the concentration of Mexicans who have come from an area in Mexico called Puebla. [90]

Not all Puerto Ricans, especially those who had grown up in El Barrio, were happy about the change. They missed El Barrio of their childhoods with its hand-painted murals, the sounds of salsa music, the pickup games of dominoes on the sidewalks, and the pushcart vendors selling *piraguas* (snow cones). They wanted to reclaim their heritage by revitalizing the neighborhood they had grown up in, the neighborhood that had once been considered the cradle of the community.

Those who returned had a specific mission in mind. According to *New York Times* journalist Joseph Berger, "Their movement, the returnees say, is a philosophical crusade to keep Spanish Harlem the Puerto Rican heartland in the United States. . . . [Those

Where Most Puerto Rican Americans Live in the USA

Springfield, MA
35,251

Chicago, IL
113,055

Hartford, CT
39,586

Bridgeport, CT
30,250

New York, NY
789,172

Newark, NJ
39,650

Philadelphia, PA
91,527

Miami, FL
85,000

States with the largest number of Puerto Rican American residents

● Cities in which more than 30,000 Puerto Rican Americans live

Major areas where most Puerto Rican Americans live

According to the 2000 U.S. Census, there are more than 3.4 million Puerto Ricans living in the mainland United States, with the majority living on the East Coast. Puerto Ricans make up 1.2% of the total U.S. population.

who returned] saw a neighborhood that was rapidly losing the accent and influence that had defined it."[91] As Puerto Ricans began returning to El Barrio, the neighborhood's once decrepit and abandoned buildings were being refurbished and art galleries, trendy restaurants, and new apartment buildings began springing up.

This change was a welcome sight for those Puerto Ricans who had returned, such as David and Betty Cutié. When their daughter was young, the Cutiés had left El Barrio

Memories of El Barrio

Author and journalist Ed Morales, who grew up in El Barrio during the years of the Great Migration, made a return trip as an adult. In an article titled "Spanish Harlem on His Mind," which appeared in the New York Times, *Morales captures memories of being raised in this uniquely Puerto Rican enclave in the middle of New York City.*

El Barrio. In my childhood its mere mention conjured all kinds of feelings, from a kind of reverence for proud beginnings to my parents' wariness of its slow descent into hard times. It was a magic Spanish phrase that fell easily from my father's lips, a reference to a place that curiously seemed to belong to us, even though New York didn't belong to us. As more of us moved to various corners of the Bronx, El Barrio increasingly became the source of authenticity, like the *bacalaitos* (codfish fritters) on 116th Street that were the closest thing to what you could get on the island.

As I grew older and the neighborhood's mean streets became even meaner, I was still in awe of its self-assured Latin style. . . .

Sharkskin-suit-wearing mambo men spinning leggy lace-draped women at the Park Palace on 110th and Fifth Avenue lurked in my subconscious. Multicolored Latin men standing their ground against turf invaders, wearing T-shirts and pegged pants, with an angry curled lock of defiance spilling onto their foreheads, haunted me in my exiles in the Bronx, New England, and the Lower East Side. I could almost hear the slow boleros from rooftop parties, the anomalous screech of roosters on fire escapes, holding me in the grip of the peculiar alchemy created by tropical people shivering in poorly heated tenements.

The late theater director and promoter Eddie Figueroa, who lived in the [housing] projects at 114th and Lexington Avenue, once declared that wherever he called home was the embassy of the Spirit Republic of Puerto Rico, and for the first time I understood El Barrio as a sanctuary of an idea, an identity. It was an imaginary homeland that I shared with countless other displaced souls, U.S.-entrenched Puerto Ricans in search of being Puerto Rican.

for the suburbs. As they approached retirement age, they realized they wanted to go back to their roots. In 2001 they returned to El Barrio. However, they returned not as passive residents but as citizens who want to make a difference in their community. They are fixing up an old brownstone and David serves on East Harlem's community board. The Cutiés and those like them are starting the process of reclaiming El Barrio for future generations of Puerto Ricans.

Paseo Boricua

Just as El Barrio has undergone revitalization in recent years, so, too, has one of Chicago's largest Puerto Rican neighborhoods: La Division. For years, La Division had been the heart of Chicago's Puerto Rican community. It was home to Puerto Rican organizations such as the Teatro San Juan, Roberto Clemente High School, and several Spanish-language newspapers. However, La Division had a somewhat tarnished reputation. When Nilda Flores-González first visited it in 1989, she encountered both the positive and negative aspects of the neighborhood:

I was immediately transported to my childhood and adolescent days in Río Piedras [Puerto Rico]. Similar sounds and smells surrounded me as a child. I immediately felt connected to "La Division," yet I remained cautious because "La Division" had a bad reputation. . . . Sidewalks were in bad shape and empty lots were unkept and strewn with trash. Drug activity was routine and one could see drug transactions in daylight,

as well as find used needles littering sidewalks. I was told repeatedly not to attend the *Fiestas Patronales* (Puerto Rican Festivities) at the park because "there is always shooting."[92]

In the meantime, Chicago's leaders wanted to lure wealthy citizens back into the heart of the city. They did this by cleaning up poor areas such as La Division and replacing dilapidated homes and apartment buildings with expensive luxury homes. While this drew many wealthy Chicagoans back into the city, the high rents had forced many ethnic groups to leave. Puerto Rican leaders refused to let this happen to La Division and began taking action.

The results of their effort were stunning. When Flores-González returned in 1995, she was amazed by the results. Community leaders had reshaped La Division from a disorganized, dangerous area into a neat, orderly outgrowth of Puerto Rican culture known as Paseo Boricua. It is a mile-long stretch along Division Street, flanked by two large Puerto Rican flags at each of its two entry points, that showcases Puerto Rican businesses and cultural centers. According to some Puerto Rican residents of the neighborhood, the area is becoming *un Viejo San Juan con nieve* (an Old San Juan with snow).

Migration in the Twenty-First Century

In the twenty-first century Puerto Rican migration has been transformed. Today's migrants stand in stark contrast to those who arrived just fifty years before. No longer are the majority of migrants unskilled workers who

Among the professional Puerto Rican Americans who moved to the United States in search of greater opportunities is Antonia Novello, who served as George H.W. Bush's surgeon general from 1990 to 1993.

are forced to flee their beloved island for low-level jobs on the mainland. Instead, the migrants who choose to leave their island are highly educated. For them, moving to the United States is a way to advance their careers.

Though sad to leave Puerto Rico, many migrants believe the small island cannot provide the same opportunities the United States can. "You can get a master's degree and wind up working [as a clerk] in Plaza las Americas mall [in Puerto Rico]," says Aida Giachello, an associate professor at the University of Illinois at Chicago.[93] John López-Haage, who earned his degree as an engineer in Puerto Rico, moved to the United States with his wife and three children for that very reason. "There were not too many opportunities back in Puerto Rico," says López-Haage. "A lot of our

friends—doctors and artists—also have moved to the states."[94]

López-Haage is not alone. Each year, thousands of doctors, professors, engineers, and computer scientists are traveling to the United States. Like the generations of migrants who came before them, these Puerto Ricans are about to embark on a new journey that will challenge every aspect of their lives, from their professional skills to their very identity. However, they take on these challenges not as something to fear but rather as a set of opportunities to be embraced. "We were American citizens before we ever set foot in the United States. That made us unique among immigrants. So, we had two loyalties and two very powerful loves," says Puerto Rican–born actor Raúl Dávila. "It was not easy, but we always had the possibility of making the best of both worlds."[95]

NOTES

Introduction: The Puerto Rican Experience

1. Quoted in Elissa Gootman, "The Day That Fifth Avenue Runs All the Way to San Juan," *New York Times,* June 9, 2003, p. B1.
2. Quoted in Edward Mapp, ed., *Puerto Rican Perspectives.* Metuchen, NJ: Scarecrow Press, 1974, p. v.
3. Quoted in Sam Toperoff, *The Puerto Ricans: Our American Story.* Plainview: NY, WLIW21 Public Television, 1999.

Chapter One: The Pioneer Migration

4. Quoted in Juan González, *Harvest of Empire: A History of Latinos in America.* New York: Viking, 2000, p. 62.
5. Quoted in Bernardo Vega, *Memoirs of Bernardo Vega: A Contribution to the History of the Puerto Rican Community in New York,* trans. Juan Flores. New York: Monthly Review Press, 1984, p. 89.
6. Vega, *Memoirs of Bernardo Vega,* pp. 5–6.
7. Quoted in *Magazine of History,* "Old Voices, New Voices: Mainland Puerto Rican Perspectives and Experiences," 10, no. 2 (Winter 1996). www.oah.org/pubs/magazine/Latinos/Old%20voices.html.
8. *New York Times,* "Ask Police Protection: New York Porto Ricans Complain of Being Attacked," July 30, 1926, p. 29.
9. Vega, *Memoirs of Bernardo Vega,* p. 32.
10. Quoted in Virginia E. Sánchez Korrol, *From Colonia to Community: The History of Puerto Ricans in New York City.* Berkeley and Los Angeles: University of California Press, 1994, p. 109.
11. Ronald Fernández, *The Disenchanted Island: Puerto Rico and the United States in the Twentieth Century.* New York: Praeger, 1992, p. 66.
12. Quoted in Kal Wagenheim and Olga Jiménez de Wagenheim, eds., *The Puerto Ricans: A Documentary History.* Princeton, NJ: Markus Wiener, 1994, p. 168.
13. Quoted in Raymond Carr, *Puerto Rico: A Colonial Experiment.* New York: New York University Press, 1984, p. 62.
14. Quoted in Lawrence R. Chenault, *The Puerto Rican Migrant in New York City.* 1938. Reprint, New York: Russell & Russell, 1970, p. 81.
15. Quoted in Chenault, *The Puerto Rican Migrant in New York City,* p. 81.
16. Quoted in Vega, *Memoirs of Bernardo Vega,* p. 210.

Chapter Two: The Great Migration

17. Quoted in Sánchez Korrol, *From Colonia to Community,* p. 44.
18. Quoted in Sánchez Korrol, *From Colonia to Community,* p. 44.
19. Wagenheim and Wagenheim, *The Puerto Ricans,* p. 183.
20. Quoted in Carmen Teresa Whalen, *From Puerto Rico to Philadelphia: Puerto Rican Workers and Postwar Economics.* Philadelphia: Temple University Press, 2001, p. 36.

21. Quoted in Whalen, *From Puerto Rico to Philadelphia,* p. 49.

22. Quoted in Roland I. Perusse, *The United States and Puerto Rico: The Struggle for Equality.* Malabar, FL: Robert E. Krieger, 1990, p. 114.

23. Quoted in Perusse, *The United States and Puerto Rico,* p. 116.

24. Quoted in Christopher Rand, *The Puerto Ricans.* New York: Oxford University Press, 1958, pp. 53–54.

25. Peter Kihss, "Puerto Rico Combats Exodus by a Drive to Raise Incomes," *New York Times,* February 24, 1953, p. 1.

26. Quoted in Oscar Lewis, *A Study of Slum Culture: Backgrounds for La Vida.* New York: Random House, 1968, p. 125.

27. Quoted in Lewis, *A Study of Slum Culture,* pp. 126–27.

28. Quoted in Lewis, *A Study of Slum Culture,* p. 127

29. Quoted in Rand, *The Puerto Ricans,* p. 68.

30. Quoted in Sánchez Korrol, *From Colonia to Community,* p. 93.

31. Matthew Hay Brown, "Influence on the Mainland," *Hartford Courant,* July 22, 2002, p. A5.

32. Clayton Knowless, "Five Congressmen Shot in House by 3 Puerto Rican Nationalists," *New York Times,* March 2, 1954, p. 1.

33. Quoted in Edna Acosta-Belén et al., *Adiós, Borinquen Querida: The Puerto Rican Diaspora, Its History and Contributions.* Albany, NY: Center for Latino, Latin American, and Caribbean Studies, 2000, p. 38.

Chapter Three: The "Puerto Rican Problem"

34. Peter Kihss, "Puerto Rican Will to Work Stressed," *New York Times,* February 25, 1953, p. 18.

35. Esmeralda Santiago, *When I Was Puerto Rican.* Reading, MA: Addison-Wesley, 1993, pp. 249–50.

36. Quoted in Rand, *The Puerto Ricans,* p. 112.

37. González, *Harvest of Empire,* pp. 90–91.

38. Quoted in Rand, *The Puerto Ricans,* p. 15.

39. Quoted in Dan Wakefield, "The Other Puerto Ricans," *New York Times,* October 11, 1959, p. SM24.

40. Quoted in Wakefield, "The Other Puerto Ricans," p. SM24.

41. Charles Abrams, "How to Remedy Our 'Puerto Rican Problem,'" *Commentary* 19, no. 2 (February 1955): 122.

42. Quoted in Rand, *The Puerto Ricans,* pp. 100–101.

43. Santiago, *When I Was Puerto Rican,* p. 73.

44. Quoted in Historical Society of Pennsylvania, "Post-WWII Migration." www.hsp.org/default.aspx?id=362.

45. Quoted in Leslie Postal and Tania de-Luzuriaga, "Teaching English to Puerto Ricans Is Put to Test," *Orlando Sentinel,* April 26, 2004, p. A1.

46. Maura I. Toro-Morn, "Yo Era Muy Arriesgada: A Historical Overview of the Work Experiences of Puerto Rican Women in Chicago," *Centro Journal* 13, no. 2 (Fall 2001): 34.

47. Quoted in Gina M. Pérez, "An Upbeat West Side Story: Puerto Ricans and Postwar Racial Politics in Chicago," *Centro Journal* 13, no. 2 (Fall 2001): 47.

48. Quoted in *New York Times,* "Puerto Ricans Win Praise as Citizens," February 17, 1952, p. 56.

49. Quoted in *New York Times,* "Defends Puerto Ricans," June 12, 1955, p. 15.

Chapter Four: The Revolving Door

50. Quoted in Rand, *The Puerto Ricans,* p. 57.

51. Quoted in A.W. Maldonado, "The Puerto Rican Tide Begins to Turn," *New York Times,* September 20, 1964, p. SM84.

52. Quoted in Perusse, *The United States and Puerto Rico,* p. 43.

53. Quoted in Mervin Méndez, "A Community Fights Back: Recollections of the 1966 Division Street Riot," *Diálogo* no. 2, (Winter/Spring 1998). http://condor.depaul.edu/~dialogo/back_issues/issue_2/community_fights_back.htm.

54. Félix M. Padilla, *Puerto Rican Chicago.* Notre Dame, IN: University of Notre Dame Press, 1987, p. 121.

55. Quoted in Juan M. Vásquez, "Many from Puerto Rico Flee City for Homeland," *New York Times,* February 8, 1972, p. 1.

56. William Stockton, "Going Home: The Puerto Ricans' New Migration," *New York Times,* November 12, 1978, p. SM15.

57. Quoted in Stockton, "Going Home: The Puerto Ricans' New Migration," p. SM15.

58. Quoted in Carlos Antonio Torre, Hugo Rodríguez Vecchini, and William Burgos, eds., *The Commuter Nation: Perspectives on Puerto Rican Migration.* Río Piedras, PR: Editorial de la Universidad de Puerto Rico, 1994, p. 307.

59. Quoted in Tom Lowry, "From Island to Mainland and Back," Allentown (Pennsylvania) *Morning Call,* December 8, 1988, p. A1.

60. Quoted in Jeff Kunerth, "Return to Puerto Rico Completes Cycle of Life," *Orlando Sentinel,* November 30, 2002, p. A1.

61. Quoted in Kunerth, "Return to Puerto Rico Completes Cycle of Life," p. A1.

62. Quoted in Edgar Sandoval, "Natives Return to Their Enchanted Island," *Morning Call,* July 21, 2002, p. S6.

Chapter Five: A Juggling Act

63. Quoted in Toperoff, *The Puerto Ricans.*

64. Sonia Nieto, "On Becoming American: An Exploratory Essay," *Masterpiece Theatre.* www.pbs.org/wgbh/masterpiece/americancollection/woman/ei_puertoricans_nieto.html.

65. Nieto, "On Becoming American: An Exploratory Essay."

66. Quoted in Veronica Chambers et al., "Latino America," *Newsweek,* July 12, 1999, p. 50.

67. Luisita López Torregrosa, *The Noise of Infinite Longing: A Memoir of a Family and an Island.* New York: Rayo/HarperCollins, 2004, p. 159.

68. Quoted in Frances Negrón-Muntaner, *Boricua Pop: Puerto Ricans and the Latinization of American Culture.* New York: New York University Press, 2004, p. 59.

69. Negrón-Muntaner, *Boricua Pop,* p. 58.

70. Quoted in Jorge Duany, *The Puerto Rican Nation on the Move.* Chapel Hill: University of North Carolina Press, 2002, p. 195.

71. Quoted in Toperoff, *The Puerto Ricans.*
72. Quoted in Duany, *The Puerto Rican Nation on the Move,* p. 193.
73. Quoted in Alan Feuer, "Bronx Haven Is Threatened, but Denizens Still Dream," *New York Times,* September 26, 2003, p. B1.
74. Robert Friedman, "Language Purists Dismayed by Spanglish," *Star-Tribune,* January 24, 2001, p. E1.
75. Quoted in Rand, *The Puerto Ricans,* p. 25.
76. Quoted in Deborah Kong, "Spanglish Creeps into Mainstream," *Lincoln Journal Star,* November 4, 2002, p. 8.
77. Quoted in Ricardo Alonso-Zaldivar, "For Millions of Latinos, Race Is a Flexible Concept," *Los Angeles Times,* March 11, 2003, p. A1.
78. Duany, *The Puerto Rican Nation on the Move,* p. 255.
79. Quoted in Brown, "Influence on the Mainland," p. A5.
80. Quoted in CNN.com, "Puerto Ricans Say 'No' to Statehood," December 14, 1998. www.cnn.com/US/9812/14/puerto.rico.01/.

Chapter Six: An American Success Story

81. Quoted in Mapp, *Puerto Rican Perspectives,* p. 53.
82. Quoted in Albor Ruiz, "Hailing Latino Paper of Record," *New York Daily News,* June 19, 2003, p. 3.
83. Quoted in Acosta-Belén et al., *Adiós, Borinquen Querida,* p. 145; translation provided by author.
84. Quoted in Sandra Bailey, "Go Ahead, Ask Gigi Fernández Why She's Playing for the United States," *Chicago Tribune,* August 9, 1992, p. 16.
85. Quoted in SNL Financial, "Popular, Inc. Became the First Puerto Rican Financial Company to Open the NASDAQ Stock Market." www.snl.com/Interactive/IR/file.asp?IID=100165&FID=1502238&OSID=9.
86. Quoted in Nancy Jo Sales, "Vida Lopez," *New York Magazine,* September 6, 1999. www.newyorkmetro.com/nymetro/news/culture/features/1395/index.html.
87. Quoted in Craig Horowitz, "Rebuilding the Barrio," *New York Magazine,* September 6, 1999. www.newyorkmetro.com/nymetro/news/culture/features/1397/index.html.
88. Quoted in Fernanda Santos, "Puerto Ricans Take Road to a Better Life: Middle Class Leaving City for Suburbs," *New York Daily News,* August 10, 2003, p. 8.
89. Quoted in Santos, "Puerto Ricans Take Road to a Better Life," p. 8.
90. Horowitz, "Rebuilding the Barrio."
91. Joseph Berger, "After Exodus, Gentrification Changes Face of East Harlem," *New York Times,* December 10, 2002, p. B1.
92. Nilda Flores-González, "Paseo Boricua: Claiming a Puerto Rican Space in Chicago," *Centro Journal* 13, no. 2 (Fall 2001): 8.
93. Quoted in Teresa Puente, "A New Migration," *Chicago Tribune,* August 16, 1998, p. 1.
94. Quoted in Puente, "A New Migration," p. 1.
95. Quoted in Toperoff, *The Puerto Ricans.*

FOR FURTHER READING

Books

Jerome J. Aliotta and Sandra Stotsky, *The Puerto Ricans.* New York: Chelsea House, 1996. This book, which is part of the Immigrant Experience series, covers a variety of topics related to Puerto Rican migrants including assimilation, history, and culture.

Jesús Colón, *A Puerto Rican in New York and Other Sketches,* 2nd ed. New York: International Publishers, 1982. Colón, a Puerto Rican who arrived in New York in 1918 as a stowaway on a ship, reveals what life was like in the city during the years of the Pioneer Migration. He tells his story through poignant and sometimes humorous vignettes.

Judith Harlan, *Puerto Rico: Deciding Its Future.* New York: Twenty-First Century Books, 1996. This book provides background on Puerto Rico's history, as well as reasons for migration and what life is like for Puerto Ricans on the mainland. It also delves into the complex notions of statehood, independence, or commonwealth status for the island.

Robert L. Muckley and Adela Martínez-Santiago, *Stories from Puerto Rico.* Lincolnwood, IL: Passport Books, 1999. This bilingual book presents eighteen traditional stories and legends from Puerto Rico, including the Taíno creation story and well-known folktales such as Juan Bobo.

Piri Thomas, *Down These Mean Streets,* 30th Anniversary ed. New York: Vintage Books, 1997. The memoir of Piri Thomas, an American-born man of Puerto Rican and Cuban descent, explores the raw and oftentimes disturbing realities of discrimination, crime, and drugs present in the Spanish Harlem of his youth.

Web Sites

Mi Barrio (www.mibarrio.org). This site provides information on Spanish Harlem, including photographs, neighborhood demographics, and current events.

Puerto Rico and the American Dream (www.prdream.com). This award-winning site features photographs and oral histories of migrants in Spanish and English. It also provides profiles of Puerto Ricans who have become famous in the United States.

Puerto Rico Herald (www.puertorico herald.org). The *Puerto Rico Herald* is the definitive source for news regarding Puerto Rico and Puerto Ricans in the United States. It features stories in Spanish and English that cover topics from citizenship and culture to the status debate and current events.

WORKS CONSULTED

Books

Edna Acosta-Belén et al., *Adiós, Borinquen Querida: The Puerto Rican Diaspora, Its History and Contributions.* Albany, NY: Center for Latino, Latin American, and Caribbean Studies, 2000. The book traces the migration experiences, as well as the influence Puerto Ricans have had on the media, literature, the arts, politics, and science.

Raymond Carr, *Puerto Rico: A Colonial Experiment.* New York: New York University Press, 1984. A scholarly overview of Puerto Rico after the Spanish-American War.

Lawrence R. Chenault, *The Puerto Rican Migrant in New York City.* 1938. Reprint, New York: Russell & Russell, 1970. Provides some of the earliest analysis of Puerto Ricans who arrived in New York City during the Pioneer Migration.

Jorge Duany, *The Puerto Rican Nation on the Move.* Chapel Hill: University of North Carolina Press, 2002. Examines the cultural identities of Puerto Ricans and the island's diaspora.

August A. Failde and William S. Doyle, *Latino Success: Insights from 100 of America's Most Powerful Latino Business Professionals.* New York: Simon & Schuster, 1996. Offers personal stories as well as advice from leaders in the Latino community who have been successful in the business world.

Ronald Fernández, *The Disenchanted Island: Puerto Rico and the United States in the Twentieth Century.* New York: Praeger, 1992. This book presents the complex relationship between Puerto Rico and the United States in the twentieth century.

Juan Flores, *From Bomba to Hip-Hop: Puerto Rican Culture and Latino Identity.* New York: Columbia University Press, 2000. A study of Puerto Rican culture and identity in the United States, with a special emphasis on the role that music has played in these communities and its influence on mainstream America.

Juan González, *Harvest of Empire: A History of Latinos in America.* New York: Viking, 2000. An overview of Latin Americans in the United States throughout history.

Oscar Lewis, *A Study of Slum Culture: Backgrounds for La Vida.* New York: Random House, 1968. An in-depth look at the conditions Puerto Rican migrants encountered in New York City. The book includes numerous interviews as well as objective analysis of housing conditions, family size, occupations, and public relief.

Edward Mapp, ed., *Puerto Rican Perspectives.* Metuchen, NJ: Scarecrow Press, 1974. A collection of essays of different aspects about Puerto Rican assimilation.

Ed Morales, *Living in Spanglish: The Search for Latino Identity in America.* New York: St. Martin's Press, 2002. An in-depth look at how Puerto Ricans, as well as others in America's Latino communities, fuse their Latino and American identities.

Frances Negrón-Muntaner, *Boricua Pop: Puerto Ricans and the Latinization of American Culture.* New York: New York University Press, 2004. An in-depth, current look at the way Puerto Rican migrants have influenced American culture from *West Side Story* to Jennifer Lopez.

New York University, Graduate School of Public Administration and Social Service, *The Impact of Puerto Rican Migration on Governmental Services in New York City*. New York: New York University Press, 1957. A scholarly look at how Puerto Rican migrants impacted New York City during the early years of the Great Migration.

Elena Padilla, *Up from Puerto Rico*. New York: Columbia University Press, 1958. Padilla, an anthropologist, reveals her findings and analysis after spending two-and-a-half years studying life in a Puerto Rican neighborhood on the mainland.

Félix M. Padilla, *Puerto Rican Chicago*. Notre Dame, IN: University of Notre Dame Press, 1987. A scholarly history of the Puerto Rican community living in Chicago.

Antonia Pantoja, *Memoir of a Visionary: Antonia Pantoja*. Houston, TX: Arte Público Press, 2002. Pantoja, a Puerto Rican American activist and community leader, describes her life and experiences on the island and mainland.

María E. Pérez y González, *Puerto Ricans in the United States*. Westport, CT: Greenwood Press, 2000. Pérez y González covers island history, stages of migration, and migrant experiences ranging from religion to economics.

Roland I. Perusse, *The United States and Puerto Rico: The Struggle for Equality*. Malabar, FL: Robert E. Krieger, 1990. A history of Puerto Rico, including an anthology of primary source materials, with an emphasis on government.

Christopher Rand, *The Puerto Ricans*. New York: Oxford University Press, 1958.

An overview of the Puerto Rican community in New York during the years of the Great Migration.

Virginia E. Sánchez Korrol, *From Colonia to Community: The History of Puerto Ricans in New York City*. Berkeley and Los Angeles: University of California Press, 1994. This book traces the establishment of New York City's Puerto Rican community during the twentieth century, with an emphasis on the Pioneer and Great Migrations.

Esmeralda Santiago, *When I Was Puerto Rican*. Reading, MA: Addison-Wesley, 1993. A memoir of a Puerto Rican migrant who arrived in Brooklyn in 1961.

Ilan Stavans, *Spanglish: The Making of a New American Language*. New York: Rayo/HarperCollins, 2003. Stavans explores the concept of Spanglish and how it fits into American society in the twenty-first century. He also includes an exhaustive "Lexicon" section, with examples of Spanglish terms and usage.

Carlos Antonio Torre, Hugo Rodríguez Vecchini, and William Burgos, eds., *The Commuter Nation: Perspectives on Puerto Rican Migration*. Río Piedras, PR: Editorial de la Universidad de Puerto Rico, 1994. A collection of scholarly essays surrounding the Revolving-Door Migration patterns and their effects on the migrants as well as the mainland and island communities.

Luisita López Torregrosa, *The Noise of Infinite Longing: A Memoir of a Family and an Island*. New York: Rayo/HarperCollins, 2004. The memoir of López Torregrosa, who grew up in a privileged family, recalls her life and times on the island as well as her experiences after she arrived in the United States to attend a boarding school as a teenager.

Bernardo Vega, *Memoirs of Bernardo Vega: A Contribution to the History of the Puerto Rican Community in New York,* trans. Juan Flores. New York: Monthly Review Press, 1984. The memoirs of Puerto Rican migrant Bernardo Vega provide a firsthand account of New York City in the early 1900s, as well as an in-depth historical perspective on early Puerto Rican migration.

Kal Wagenheim and Olga Jiménez de Wagenheim, eds., *The Puerto Ricans: A Documentary History.* Princeton, NJ: Markus Wiener, 1994. An anthology of primary source materials relating to Puerto Rico's history and to the experiences of Puerto Ricans living in the United States.

Dan Wakefield, *Island in the City: The World of Spanish Harlem.* Boston, MA: Houghton Mifflin, 1959. Wakefield, a journalist, recounts the experiences of Puerto Rican migrants from the journey to the mainland to daily life in New York City.

Carmen Teresa Whalen, *From Puerto Rico to Philadelphia: Puerto Rican Workers and Postwar Economics.* Philadelphia: Temple University Press, 2001. Whalen's book takes a scholarly look at migrants who left Puerto Rico after World War II and settled in Pennsylvania. It covers a broad range of topics from discrimination and poverty to contract laborers and assimilation.

Periodicals

Alex Abella, "From the Young Lords to the Mainstream," *Los Angeles Times,* April 1, 2001, p. E1.

Charles Abrams, "How to Remedy Our 'Puerto Rican Problem,'" *Commentary* 19, no. 2 (February 1955): 120–27.

Albany (New York) *Times Union,* "Puerto Rican Barbie Goes Into Politics," November 30, 1997, p. G6.

Ricardo Alonso-Zaldivar, "For Millions of Latinos, Race Is a Flexible Concept," *Los Angeles Times,* March 11, 2003, p. A1.

Sandra Bailey, "Go Ahead, Ask Gigi Fernández Why She's Playing for the United States," *Chicago Tribune,* August 9, 1992, p. 16.

Joseph Berger, "After Exodus, Gentrification Changes Face of East Harlem," *New York Times,* December 10, 2002, p. B1.

Matthew Hay Brown, "Influence on the Mainland," *Hartford Courant,* July 22, 2002, p. A5.

Veronica Chambers et al., "Latino America," *Newsweek,* July 12, 1999, pp. 48–51.

Chicago Tribune, "Puerto Ricans Say 'No' to Statehood," November 15, 1993, p. 1.

George Diaz, "Clemente 30 Years After His Tragic Death," *Orlando Sentinel,* March 31, 2002, p. BB2.

Alan Feuer, "Bronx Haven Is Threatened, but Denizens Still Dream," *New York Times,* September 26, 2003, p. B1.

Nilda Flores-González, "Paseo Boricua: Claiming a Puerto Rican Space in Chicago," *Centro Journal* 13, no 2 (Fall 2001): 7–23.

Robert Friedman, "Language Purists Dismayed by Spanglish," Minneapolis *Star-Tribune,* January 24, 2001, p. E1.

Elissa Gootman, "The Day That Fifth Avenue Runs All the Way to San Juan," *New York Times,* June 9, 2003, p. B1.

Charles Grutzner, "City Puerto Ricans: Complex Problem," *New York Times,* October 3, 1949, p. 11.

———, "Teen Gangs Spawned by Longing for Friends," *New York Times,* May 13, 1955, p. 27.

Leslie Highley, "Puerto Rican Migration," *New York Times,* February 27, 1953, p. 20.

Ron Howell, "In the Market for Economic Growth," *Newsday,* November 9, 2003, p. A7.

Peter Kihss, "Flow of Puerto Ricans Here Fills Jobs, Poses Problems," *New York Times,* February 23, 1953, p. 1.

———, "Puerto Rican Will to Work Stressed," *New York Times,* February 25, 1953, p. 18.

———, "Puerto Rico Combats Exodus by a Drive to Raise Incomes," *New York Times,* February 24, 1953, p. 1.

Clayton Knowless, "Five Congressmen Shot in House by 3 Puerto Rican Nationalists," *New York Times,* March 2, 1954, p. 1.

Deborah Kong, "Spanglish Creeps into Mainstream," *Lincoln (Nebraska) Journal Star,* November 4, 2002, p. 8.

Jeff Kunerth, "Return to Puerto Rico Completes Cycle of Life," *Orlando Sentinel,* November 30, 2002, p. A1.

Tom Lowry, "From Island to Mainland and Back," Allentown (Pennsylvania) *Morning Call,* December 8, 1988, p. A1.

A.W. Maldonado, "The Puerto Rican Tide Begins to Turn," *New York Times,* September 20, 1964, p. SM84.

Ed Morales, "Spanish Harlem on His Mind," *New York Times,* February 23, 2003, p. CY1.

Mireya Navarro, "A New Barbie in Puerto Rico Divides Island and Mainland," *New York Times,* December 27, 1997, p. 1.

New York Times, "Ask, Police Protection: New York Porto Ricans Complain of Being Attacked," July 30, 1926, p. 29.

———, "Defends Puerto Ricans," June 12, 1955, p. 15.

———, "Island Is Often Hit by Severe Storms," September 28, 1932, p. 3.

———, "Puerto Ricans Win Praise as Citizens," February 17, 1952, p. 56.

Gina M. Pérez, "An Upbeat West Side Story: Puerto Ricans and Postwar Racial Politics in Chicago," *Centro Journal* 13, no. 2 (Fall 2001): 47–71.

Leslie Postal and Tania deLuzuriaga, "Teaching English to Puerto Ricans Is Put to Test," *Orlando Sentinel,* April 26, 2004, p. A1.

Teresa Puente, "A New Migration," *Chicago Tribune,* August 16, 1998, p. 1.

Ray Quintanilla, "Painful Memories Leave Many Residents Suspicious of English Lessons," *Orlando Sentinel,* May 2, 2004, p. A18.

Ana Y. Ramos-Zayas, "Delinquent Citizenship, National Performances: Racialization, Surveillance, and the Politics of 'Worthiness' in Puerto Rican Chicago," *Latino Studies,* no. 2 (2004): 26–44.

Albor Ruiz, "Hailing Latino Paper of Record," *New York Daily News,* June 19, 2003, p. 3.

Edgar Sandoval, "Natives Return to Their Enchanted Island," Allentown (Pennsylvania) *Morning Call,* July 21, 2002, p. S6.

Fernanda Santos, "Puerto Ricans Take Road to a Better Life: Middle Class Leaving City for Suburbs," *New York Daily News,* August 10, 2003, p. 8.

William Stockton, "Going Home: The Puerto Ricans' New Migration," *New York Times,* November 12, 1978, p. SM15.

———, "Puerto Rico: A Dream Divided," *New York Times,* November 4, 1984, p. 339.

Maura I. Toro-Morn, "Yo Era Muy Arriesgada: A Historical Overview of the Work Experiences of Puerto Rican Women in Chicago," *Centro Journal* 13, no. 2 (Fall 2001): 25–43.

Juan M. Vásquez, "Many from Puerto Rico Flee City for Homeland," *New York Times,* February 8, 1972, p. 1.

Dan Wakefield, "The Other Puerto Ricans," *New York Times,* October 11, 1959, p. SM24.

Video

Sam Toperoff, *The Puerto Ricans: Our American Story.* Plainview: NY, WLIW21 Public Television, 1999. An overview of the Puerto Rican experience in the United States based on interviews with influential Puerto Ricans such as Rita Moreno, Jimmy Smits, Tito Puente, and Esmeralda Santiago.

Internet Sources

Hisham Aidi, "Exhibitions Celebrate Afro-Puerto Rican Heritage." Africana: Your Gateway to the Black World. www.africana.com/articles/daily/index_20001119.asp.

Helen G. Chapin, "Puerto Ricans Arrive in Hawaii," The Hawaiian Historical Society, 1994. http://www.hawaiianhistory.org/pr.html.

CNN.com. "Puerto Ricans Say 'No' to Statehood," December 14, 1998. www.cnn.com/US/9812/14/puerto.rico.01/.

Global Security, "1st Battalion–65th Infantry Regiment." www.globalsecurity.org/military/agency/army/1-65in.htm.

Historical Society of Pennsylvania, "Post-WWII Migration." www.hsp.org/default.aspx?id=362.

Craig Horowitz, "Rebuilding the Barrio," *New York Magazine,* September 6, 1999. www.newyorkmetro.com/nymetro/news/culture/features/1397/index.html.

Latino Education Network Service, "About Young Lords." http://palante.org/AboutYoung Lords.htm.

Magazine of History, "Old Voices, New Voices: Mainland Puerto Rican Perspectives and Experiences," 10, no. 2 (Winter 1996). www.oah.org/pubs/magazine/Latinos/Old%20voices.html.

Mervin Méndez, "A Community Fights Back: Recollections of the 1966 Division Street Riot," *Diálogo* no. 2 (Winter/Spring 1998). http://condor.depaul.edu/~dialogo/back_issues/issue_2/community_fights_back.htm.

Sonia Nieto, "On Becoming American: An Exploratory Essay," *Masterpiece Theatre.* www.pbs.org/wgbh/masterpiece/americancollection/woman/ei_puerto ricans_nieto.html.

Puerto Rico Herald, "Puerto Rico Profile: Rita Moreno." August 10, 2000. www.puertorico-herald.org/issues/vol4n32/Profile Moreno-en.shtml.

Nancy Jo Sales, "Vida Lopez," *New York Magazine,* September 6, 1999. www.new yorkmetro.com/nymetro/news/culture/features/1395/index.html.

SNL Financial, "Popular, Inc. Became the First Puerto Rican Financial Company to Open the NASDAQ Stock Market." www.snl.com/Interactive/IR/file.asp?IID=100165&FID=1502238&OSID=9.

Robert Waddell, "New York Puerto Ricans Reclaiming Indigenous Roots." *Puerto Rico Herald,* July 12, 2000. www.puertorico-herald.org/issues/vol4n31/Taino-en.shtml.

INDEX

PICTURE CREDITS

About the Author

Kate A. Conley is a freelance editor and writer. During the course of her career, she has edited more than five hundred nonfiction manuscripts for children and written twenty nonfiction titles for the lower and middle grades. Kate graduated from the University of Minnesota with degrees in English and Spanish and has traveled in Latin America and Spain. Today, she lives in Golden Valley, Minnesota, with her husband, Vincent.